The Skye Revivals

Steve Taylor

D1381943

New Wine Press

New Wine Press
PO Box 17
Chichester
England PO20 6YB

ISBN 1 903725 26 7

Typeset by CRB Associates, Reepham, Norfolk.
Printed in England by Clays Ltd, St Ives plc.

This book is an abridgement of a much larger work by the author. The original manuscript contains the full text of all chapters, additional chapters, source references and photographs.

While the full manuscript is not available in book form a professionally produced multi media CD containing all of the above can be purchased by contacting the author at:

'Shennachie'
Kensaleyre
Isle of Skye
Scotland
IV51 9XF

Tel: +44 (0)1470 532485
Email: Steve@Skye2000.freeserve.co.uk

Alternatively visit the Skye Revivals web site on:

skyerevival.org.uk

About the author

Steve Taylor lives in Kensaleyre on the Isle of Skye with his wife Johanna and their four children.

Steve, a serving Police Officer, has worked in different parts of the Highlands and Islands where he has been associated with various Churches and Christian groups.

For the past seven years Steve has researched and written on the history of spiritual awakenings on the Isle of Skye and has produced a series of magazines entitled *Skye Revival*, as well as a number of related publications.

This is Steve's first book, written with the desire of creating a fresh hunger for the things of God in the lives of those who read it. It is also Steve's prayer that this book will challenge Christians to pray expectantly and work towards a fresh move of God in our own day and generation.

Contents

The Isle of Skye

Preface

The Isle of Skye, nestled off the West Coast of Northern Scotland, is world famous today for its stunning scenery, unique light, wildlife, history and romantic association with the legendary 'Bonnie Prince Charlie'.

However, few are aware of the events that occurred in Skye between 1800 and 1860, when the religious, social and educational face of the island was transformed as a result of spiritual awakening.

Social and economic conditions in Skye, as well as other parts of the Highlands and Islands during this period, were difficult in the extreme. Life was uncertain, the island economy was in decline, and crop failure added to the already precarious existence of the poor who made up the bulk of the population. In addition thousands of island residents were either being cruelly evicted, as landlords claimed their ancestral homes to make way for sheep, or had decided to flee their homeland in pursuit of a better life in the New World.

Between 1826 and 1827 it is estimated that over one thousand people left the island of Mull for Cape Breton while similar numbers were vacating Skye and other Hebridean Islands for the New World. In 1842 the population of Skye stood at approximately 23,000, today it fluctuates at about 10,000.

Contemporary writers, such as Donald MacLeod in his *Gloomy Memories*, would shame the state church and the majority of her Highland and Island clergy for their supporting the landowners' cruel treatment of their impoverished tenants. However, it is also an attested fact that emerging leaders in the new evangelical movement were at the forefront of opposition to the brutality inflicted upon their people.

As itinerant missionaries began traveling to the Western Highlands and Islands from Perthshire and other parts of mainland Scotland during the early years of the 19th century they faced danger and privation. Travel was difficult and dangerous and, in addition to clerical opposition, violence and robbery were a constant threat, as is evidenced by contemporary press reports.

During 1839 rumours began to circulate in the British press regarding the possible marriage of Queen Victoria, who had come to the throne on June 28th 1838, and her first cousin Prince Albert of Saxe-Coburg-Gotha. The couple were subsequently married in 1840 after Victoria had decided that as queen it was her right to propose to Albert!

While the great marriage took place in London, at the same time, in a far away part of her kingdom, the hearts of the people of Skye and her sister islands, were being won by the love of another! The result of the marriage of thousands of Hebridean folk to their beloved was subsequently to produce a vast spiritual harvest. The children of this marriage would subsequently be found in Australia, North America and in many other places throughout the world, where they would exercise a profound social and spiritual influence.

This book is an attempt to tell the story of the rise and progress of these spiritual awakenings and to trace something of their impact, both at home and abroad. Some of the facts and personalities are fairly well known, while others have been raised from historical obscurity and given, we trust, something of the place they deserve in this remarkable story.

Chapter 1

The Background

The Reformation, which affected other parts of Scotland, appears not to have touched the Isle of Skye, at least as a spiritual movement. In common with other parts of the Western Highlands and Islands the people of Skye adopted the religion of their Clan Chief or of the landed proprietors. For the most part they appear to have had little or no personal interest in vital religion.

One Skye historian noted that, following the Reformation:

> 'Nothing had been done to arouse the imagination of the people, who had been actuated in their conversion more by policy than by principal. They had discarded the old faith, but they had failed to be influenced by the new. The churches were allowed to fall in to a state of disrepair.'

As the 19th century dawned another historian described religious conditions on the island in the following terms:

> 'Druidism, Romanism and Protestantism, each contributed an element of the grotesque superstition that went under the name of religion. The island was peopled by witches, fairies, and ghosts: darkness covered the land

and gross darkness the people. Drunken and riotous excesses abounded. These were practised in connection with the most sacred events. At funerals great quantities of ardent sprits were consumed before lifting the body. The most outrageous orgies were indulged in: bagpipes were played, songs sung, filthy tales and jests recounted.'

Of the Parish of Glenelg, Ross-shire, which included the Island of Skye, it was recorded in 1805 that, in the whole Presbytery there were only two persons known as 'enlight-ened Christians'. While such statements must surely be exaggerated they do however highlight the low state of true religion. Few it is said could read the Scriptures and still fewer owned a Bible – 'in a population of many thousands not above five or six testaments could be numbered'.

In an account attributed to a 'native of Skye', the author of a document published in 1827, records:

'When a relation of mine died in 1799, I was 23 years of age; during that period I knew he lived without worship-ping God, either privately or publicly; some times he would curse or swear . . . He was an utter stranger to Jesus Christ, yet he was reckoned among the best in the parish, and of one deserving of heaven and eternal happiness, merely for his good doings . . . The parish minister said of him and another . . . that they were the most promising and sincere men in the parish. None could be found in all the parish, whose life had confor-mity to the word of God. None showed so much submission as to pray in their families; and it was said, that only two men prayed privately. And these two men were far from being serious Christians, although they were elders in the church.'

It is worthy of note, however, that one cleric writing in 1926 regarding the dearth of evangelical preaching on the island during the 18th century, states:

'According to one writer, the Gospel was not preached in the Island [Skye] before the year 1805 when Farquharson, one of the Haldane preachers, visited the Island. This is not, however, historically correct. The Rev. Neil Macvicar of St. Cuthbert's, Edinburgh, paid an annual visit to Lady Grange in the parish of Duirinish during her imprisonment there. He preached to the people in the vernacular, and the last occasion on which he did so was in 1745, when a little girl was awakened. In the Booklet, "Strange Footprints of our King," the Rev. Donald Corbet of Kinlochbervie tells the story of Mary Beaton. No one in her native Skye could give her information as to how she could become acquainted with "Jehovah" to whom it belongs "to rescue fully from death." From her home in Waternish she wandered to Inverness where she at last found rest in the knowledge of God.'

Mary Beaton or Bethune, as she is named in the source document, was an eleven-year-old girl from the parish of Duirinish on the Isle of Skye. She became concerned regarding spiritual matters, and, failing to find satisfactory answers from her parents or local minister, she travelled, as already noted, to Inverness, where she was befriended by a Christian woman who took her in to her own home. Mary, reputedly converted a short time later under the preaching of the saintly James Calder, became a Christian of repute, eventually settling in the district of Croy, near Inverness, under Calder's ministry.

Later in life Mary was instrumental in sharing the Gospel with another young Skye girl, Janet MacLeod of Kilmaluag, whom she found in Strathpeffer, Ross-shire, in circumstances similar to her own. It is said that both of these girls became women of prayer – never forgetting the spiritual darkness that covered their native island. Indeed, the Rev. Roderick MacLeod, Skye, one who, many years later, was part of the answer to their prayers, linked the days of refreshing through which he lived with the intercession of these two women.

There is little doubt that the dark picture of spiritual life in Skye generally was due, in great measure, to the inability of the population to read the Scriptures in their own language. Writing to the Gaelic School Society in Edinburgh on April 26th 1811, the Rev. Roderick MacLeod, Bracadale, reported that there was only one person in the whole parish who could read Gaelic and that he had learned to read it while in Ireland.

Writing to the same Society on July 26th 1811, the Rev. Donald Ross, Kilmuir, states:

'This parish in common with many others in the Highlands, is very destitute of religious knowledge, and of sufficient sources of instruction.'

However, this situation was about to change dramatically and, as we shall see later, the Society, to which MacLeod and Ross had written in 1811, was to be instrumental in the great educational and religious revolution which was soon to engulf the Isle of Skye.

Chapter 2

The Perthshire Connection

Perthshire and Skye might not, at first glance, appear to have much in common. However, to understand what was about to happen in Skye it is to Glen Tilt in Perthshire we must go, for it was there that John Farquharson first saw the light of day and in all probability where he experienced that all important second birth.

Little is known regarding Farquharson's background or upbringing. That he was of lowly origins there can be little doubt for he was an uneducated and simple man. What we do know, however, is that Farquharson was enrolled in one of Mr Haldane's independent preaching classes at Dundee sometime about 1800. His recommendation to this post was as a result of his 'earnest zeal and Godliness'. However, John seems not to have been suited to study, as 'his capacity for learning seemed on trial, hardly to warrant his persevering in academical studies'. Consequently, after six months, James Haldane sent him to Breadalbane, Perthshire, under the auspices of his recently formed Society for the Propagation of the Gospel at Home as 'a scripture reader amongst the poor and uneducated Highlanders'.

The Breadablane district in 1800 was destitute of any evangelical influence. There were no full Bibles in the area although a few copies of the New Testament appear to have been in circulation. The task allotted to Farquharson was far from easy. The minister of the Church of Scotland opposed him and every inn within a 32 mile radius of Loch Tay was shut against him. Only three families in the district were willing to offer him any hospitality. Despite the opposition and hardship he trecked from village to village throughout the winter of 1800–1801, reading from the Bible and sharing the good news of salvation with any who would listen.

John started his ministry in the Loch Tay area at the village of Killin on the western extremity of the loch. However, his place of meeting was soon taken from him and he made a fresh start at Ardeonaig several miles along the south shore of Loch Tay. It was here and at Ardtalnaig and Acharn that the main events of his ministry took place.

During the spring of 1801 interest began to increase and a number of people came under conviction. By early 1802 the area was in the grip of spiritual awakening and it is estimated that at least one hundred people were truly converted at that time.

John was assisted during this period by two of his converts – John Campbell, a native of Ardeonaig, who later became Pastor of the Congregational Chapel at Oban, and James Dewer, a farmer's son, who was later to become a minister at Nairn, near Inverness.

Some of those who were 'awakened' attempted to hide their condition from Farquharson and would meet in secret to encourage one another and pray. However, the local boatman told him what was going on and soon the movement became a matter of public knowledge.

An eyewitness of the events in Breadalbane describes that time:

'The manner in which many of them [the converts] were impressed was to be at first surprising – they were suddenly struck during the time of prayer; they fell to the ground, and many of them, both young and old, continued speechless for twenty minutes or half an hour ... From this place it spread to Ardeonaig and Ardtalnaig, a space of about nine miles. They all flocked together, and continued to go from house to house, praying and praising God, for eight or ten days and nights, with only two hours sleep each morning; and many of them were several nights without any sleep, busily employed conversing and comforting those who were impressed ... It was at meetings for social prayer that the most considerable awakening took place in April 1802. At one of them at Cartlehan a most extraordinary influence was felt. Fourteen persons fell down to the ground crying for mercy. Worldly business was wholly neglected, and the whole night spent in prayer and exhorting one another.'

Writing many years later Principal Daniel Dewar of Marischal College, Aberdeen (circa. 1852) described Farquharson as, 'the most wonderful man he had ever known' and says that, while he preached almost every day, 'he was remarkable in this respect, that he seldom preached without some one being awakened' ... 'I think', he continues, 'I see him still on his black pony, riding round loch Tay and from farm to farm, carrying the message of salvation to the people. Divine power accompanied his ministry. There was an awakening all round the loch. Many were brought to Christ and continued steadfast and immovable in the gospel.'

News of the revival spread through the glens and villages like wildfire. Nothing like this had ever been seen in Breadalbane before.

One of the immediate effects of this move of God was persecution. Families were divided and false reports and rumours spread in order to discredit the young believers.

Violence ensued and some of the new converts were deprived of their homes and farms. However, they bore suffering with fortitude and grace.

One young man converted under Farquharson's preaching had previously been a smuggler and poacher. He also ran an illicit still. On one occasion the Earl of Breadalbane, enquiring about the man who had so often come to his adverse attention in the past, was told, 'My Lord, he has become a missionary, and will never trouble us again'. The same man had no peace of mind until he had given his store of malt to the Excise man and handed himself in!

Farquharson himself had a brush with the law during 1802 when he was arrested for preaching in the open air in Braemar. He was consequently imprisoned in Aberdeen. However, his incarceration was short lived due to the intervention of a lawyer. During his first visit the lawyer gave John a book – *Rutherford's Letters*. Handing it to him he said, 'Read it and you will soon be liberated.' As John contemplated the suffering of the writer, he felt his own afflictions were light in comparison!

Another result of the revival in Breadalbane was the formation, at Acharn, in 1802, of a church numbering seventy members. This increased to one hundred the following year. John Farquharson was ordained as pastor with members drawn from the surrounding glens. However, a dispute of some kind arose in the congregation and Farquharson resigned in 1804, ministering thereafter, for a short time, in Killin.

One Breadalbane man in whose home Farquharson was a frequent visitor was the Grandfather of the Rev. Duncan MacGregor, famous minister of Stornoway Free Church on the Isle of Lewis. Of his mother it is recorded:

'Her young heart was powerfully impressed under Mr Farquharson's sermons, and under him she was brought to Christ. Her eyes danced for joy, and there were many manifestations of the new life that now filled her.'

As to the circumstances or route which brought this man to Skye during 1805 we know little. The reason given by one writer was that Farquharson's visit was not intentional – but that he landed from a ship as the result of some problem while on route to America. However, Rev. W.J. Couper, Glasgow, who seems to have had some direct testimony, disagrees. It is his contention that Farquharson came to Skye by design, either having been sent as a Haldane missionary or as a result of his own love of the work.

Once in Skye, John Farquharson appears to have preached first in Portree, the island capital. As he did not communicate with any of the island ministers and held meetings through the week as well as on Sunday, something of an air of novelty surrounded his preaching. Nothing quite like it had been seen or heard on the Island before. From Portree, Farquharson travelled throughout the northern part of Skye, preaching as he went. He was followed everywhere by a blind man from Portree – Donald Munro. Munro, who was subsequently converted under the preaching of John Farquharson, was to become known as the 'Father of Evangelical Religion in Skye'.

On one occasion the local parish minister of Kilmuir, Skye, Rev. Donald Martin, was passing through Uig when he happened upon Farquharson preaching to a large crowd in the open air. His text was from John 10:9: *'I am the door.'* Martin was attracted by Farquharson's zeal and earnestness and at the close of the service he invited Farquharson to his manse, where, it appears, he resided during the remainder of his stay on Skye. It has been suggested that it was as a result of his friendship with Farquharson that Martin was himself converted. Whether or not this was the case, the fact is that, although he had been the minister in Kilmuir since 1785,

Martin was not himself converted until the year Farquharson visited the island.

The full measure of the spiritual fruit borne as a result of Farquharson's visit to Skye is not known although it is believed to have been small. However, the seed that was sown during the few weeks of his visit were to burst to life within a very short period of time.

As a direct result of John Farquharson's visit Donald Munro established a prayer meeting at Snizort. It was held monthly for a period of two years and a number of people were converted. However, it was not for a further five years that revival fire was to be seen raging through the island. By that time John Farquharson had long gone and his voice had, in all probability, joined the song of worship with the saints in heaven. For, most historians appear to agree; shortly after his visit to Skye he set sail for Nova Scotia, Canada, where he died a short time later.

Chapter 3

The Blind Evangelist

Donald Munro, who was born of poor parents near Portree in 1773, was rendered blind at the age of 14 by smallpox. In order to earn a living he learned to play the violin. His musical talent and pleasant character made him a popular figure in the community around Portree.

It would appear that 33-year-old Donald first heard John Farquharson preaching at or near Uig. As the doors of the Church of Scotland were shut against the evangelist, large crowds of people gathered to hear him preach in the open air.

Donald was among the crowd who heard the preacher one day as he was expounding the text, *'I am the door; by me if any man enter in he shall be saved, and shall go in and out and find pasture.'*

Donald was later to record of Farquharson:

'I heard this worthy man four times. I believe his discourses were accompanied with divine power. From this date I got new views of Scripture myself, and of the practices of the inhabitants of the island. I think it probable that other two or three came under conviction by means of Mr Farquharson's preaching.'

Although initially only a few attended the prayer meeting

instituted by Donald, numbers gradually grew and by the first year a few people had been converted. This prayer meeting, it is said, flourished for about two years. The practice at these gatherings was for, 'two of its members to make remarks on a passage of scripture, which excited a few to prayer . . . '.

Donald, like a number of his contemporaries, revealed from time to time a supernatural knowledge of the thoughts of his listeners. On one occasion Lachlan Cameron travelled from the village of Elgol, in the south of the island, to visit friends at Snizort in the north. On Sunday, Cameron accompanied his hosts to the building where Donald Munro held his meetings. He had never heard such preaching before and mused that the speaker was mad! At that very moment Donald said, 'You are here who are saying that I am mad for telling you the truth.' Cameron was convinced Munro was indeed telling the truth, was converted and lived the rest of his life as a Christian of repute.

Another man who travelled to Snizort to hear Donald Munro was Malcolm MacRitchie – later to be the Rev. Malcolm MacRitchie of Lewis and Strathy. At the time he was a teacher at Sconser in Skye. At the end of each week he would leave Sconser and travel fifteen miles to Snizort in order to be at Donald's meetings. Later in life he noted, 'I have heard several of the Disruption worthies delivering sermons on humility, but never heard any who would come up to Donald Munro.'

As we shall see later, during the early years of the nineteenth century independent and Baptist evangelists were also active in the north of Skye. As a result of the activities of one of these evangelists, some eleven of those who attended Donald's prayer meeting were baptised by immersion.

The people from the prayer meeting who were baptised at Snizort are believed to have become the nucleus of Uig Baptist Church, which was formed about 1808.

Subsequent to these events it appears that the prayer meeting was terminated and the meetings at Snizort ceased. Some historians have attempted to put their own interpretation on these events to the detriment of the Baptist evangelists. However, there is no contemporary evidence of any dispute or ill feeling between Donald Munro and these men.

Soon after the events at Snizort, Donald appears to have turned his attention to north Skye where the Rev. Donald Martin, who, as we noted earlier, had also been influenced by John Farquharson, was the parish minister. Martin encouraged Donald and appears to have appointed him as a catechist in the area.

Donald wasted no time in setting about the task of evangelising in the Kilmuir area. In this he was assisted by a 'pious School-master from Ross-shire' whom Martin had also introduced to the area. Donald also initiated a prayer meeting in Kilmuir similar to the one he had led in Snizort. At these meetings seven or eight men would lead in prayer. Prayers were never long or laborious – but were short, earnest and devoid of repetition. Any who transgressed the rule of prayer would be rebuked – Donald Munro had no time for long pharisaic praying.

Regrettably, Donald Martin left Skye in 1808 to become the Minister of the East Church, Inverness. The people of Kilmuir sent a call to the renowned Dr John MacDonald, Ferintosh, Ross-shire. However, he declined to be their minister. A short time later MacDonald meeting Martin in Inverness, said, 'You have left the people of Kilmuir and I declined to go to them, but the Lord has raised up a blind man to minister to them, at whose feet we might sit.' The Rev. Donald Ross, a graduate of Aberdeen University, subsequently filled the Kilmuir vacancy on July 12th 1809.

A year after Ross's arrival, on June 14th 1810, Donald Munro was officially appointed as the Scottish Society for the

Prorogation of Christian Knowledge (SSPCK) catechist for the parish of Kilmuir in north Skye.

Ministerial approval of his behaviour, and compliance with his wishes, was implicit in his appointment, yet Donald was far too independent to be cowed by such restrictions and it was not long before serious differences emerged between him and the new incumbent.

For a time the Schoolmaster and Donald continued to conduct meetings in that area. Ross however was not disposed to their evangelical message and opposed them at every turn. As a result the Schoolmaster left the area in disgust. However, Donald was not for giving up continuing to hold meetings as before and, it is reported, 'great numbers' came to listen to the 'word of life'.

Donald doggedly refused to attend any of Ross's services although Ross did all he could to entice him. He once told him, 'I can break your bread for you.' Donald replied, 'Have you not read of some in the Bible who were fed by ravens with bread and flesh when no bread was left them by men?' Ross subsequently complained to the SSPCK about Donald's behaviour. A short time later, on June 12th 1812, the secretary wrote Donald in the following terms:

'Some time ago a letter was received from the Rev. Mr. Ross, your parish minister, complaining that you do not attend his ministry and thereby set a bad example to the inhabitants of the parish. You must know that the directors cannot give countenance to any of the teachers or catechists in the service of the society showing disrespect to this parish minister. I therefore hope that on reflection you will be convinced of the impropriety of your conduct ... If however you persist in refusing to attend Rev. Mr. Ross's ministrations, I am sorry to inform you that it will be impossible for you to continue in the service of the society. You will employ some friend to signify to me what you intend to do and if you determine it will be necessary for you to give over acting as catechist ... '

Donald was not dissuaded and was subsequently dismissed from his post. However, having a house in the area in which he could hold meetings, he continued his work and the people continued to flock to his meetings.

The people of Skye had an open heart to Donald. He was led by the hand from place to place or, when the situation so demanded, they carried him on their backs!

Revival came to the North of Skye about 1812, seven years after the visit of John Farquharson and the establishment, by Donald Munro, of the prayer meeting in Snizort. It began in the parish of Kilmuir where Rev. Donald Martin had laboured so faithfully and where Donald was now active. It is recorded that 'the meetings held under his [Donald Munro's] management were the means specially employed in the work'.

These meetings, which were described as 'solemn and happy occasions', are described as follows by one eyewitness:

'[They] began with praise and prayer; which were sometimes repeated in the course of the occasion, and always concluded the duties for the time. The reading of the scriptures followed the opening of the meeting – large portions of which were read aloud without note or comment. The works of such authors as were to be had in Gaelic came next.'

The 'works' referred to included books such as Boston's *Fourfold State*, Baxter's *Call*, and the writings of men such as Bunyan, Wilson, Gray and Jonathan Edwards. These books would be considered 'heavy going' by most Christians today!

The writer continues: 'Then a passage of the word of God was selected for exposition'. This task fell almost exclusively to Donald Munro. Although blind he needed no reader. It is said, 'his memory was stored with scripture and he had become, literally a living concordance'. He could recite whole chapters with ease and without the hint of error. His style was said to have been 'solemn and deeply impressive'.

Such meetings were held three times every Sunday – in open fields – in barns – or anywhere else that was available. Donald also held a weekday meeting in his own home as well as travelling to other parts of Skye for the purpose of preaching. Of these gatherings one writer commented:

> 'Their meetings were not confined to the Sabbath; and persons of discernment, who were occasionally attracted to them from the mainland, declare that they have heard poor and illiterate men guided to speak with a discrimination and force of truth, and with a spirituality of conception, scarcely to be credited, even by spiritual persons.'

'Great power', it is reported, followed such meetings between 1812 and 1814. It is said to have been common-place, just after the meeting had started and as the reader had begun for 'great meltings to come upon the hearers'. In the language of the age one writer records:

> 'Then the silent tear might be seen stealing down the rugged, but expressive, countenances turned upon the reader – the convulsive and half suppressed sigh might next be heard – female sobbings followed – and, after little, every breast was heaving under the unaccountable agitation which moved the spirits of the assembled multitudes ... Sometimes those affected cried aloud; but this was not common: at other times they threw

themselves upon the grass, in the utmost distress, and wept bitterly.'

After such services people could be seen in every direction on their knees or stretched out on the ground calling on God.

During these events even regular eating times were ignored and the people would go to extraordinary lengths to be at meetings where they could hear the Bible read. Another feature of this revival was the singing – the people did not know how to stop when they were engaged in praise! Yet another feature was that, 'The utmost cordiality and brotherly love prevailed – every man feeling his heart more tenderly drawn out to his neighbour'. There was also a great desire to testify to others as to the work God was doing. Of that work it is recorded, 'several hundred professed to have returned to the Lord, and the genuineness of their conversion was evident by the change of life that had accompanied their profession'. It was also reported 'some who had been noted for their wickedness became eminent as Christians'.

This revival was said to be 'principally confined to those not much advanced in life – of the age of fifteen, and under, to thirty'. However, there were notable exceptions, one being the conversion of an eighty-year-old man and, in the Bracadale area, a 'poor man over one hundred years'.

'Bodily agitations and crying out' were not uncommon. Some, mostly women, had dreams and visions and were said to know beforehand who were to be saved and who were not. This was considered 'marked fanaticism' by later evangelical commentators.

One church, which was formed (about 1814) in the Kilmuir area as a result of the awakening, was apparently led by a woman – Flora MacPherson, known as 'The Prophetess'. Writing for the May 1817 issue of the *Edinburgh Christian Instructor*, the Rev. Donald Ross, Kilmuir (the same man responsible for Donald Munro's dismissal from the SSPCK), was scathing of MacPherson and her followers. Regrettably his appears to be the only surviving account of this church. He noted of the group that it was:

> 'Headed up by a poor illiterate woman named Flora McPherson ... Her errors were embraced by a considerable number of the people – her wildest reveries were looked upon as divine illuminations; some of the most serious and best disposed were seduced by her imposing appearance, and viewing her in the light of one inspired, the people considered it incumbent upon them to place the most unbounded confidence in everything that dropped from the lips of one whom they believed gifted with supernatural endowments.'

He goes on to note of Flora, 'the distinguishing traits of her character were roaring, violent convulsions, high pretensions to inspiration, and communication with the Saviour ...'. However, he was also forced to concede that, 'some of both sexes who were before of abandoned lives, came at that time under serious impressions of religion which have ever remained undefaced; and to this day they continue patterns of piety, zeal, and devotedness to God'.

It is interesting to note that 'some of the most serious and best disposed' are noted as having been in fellowship with Flora. Was Donald Munro one of them? It is strange that the only record we have of this woman is one of condemnation and that from a man who also opposed Donald Munro!

Writing in 1836 of the wider awakening one commentator noted:

> 'In 1812 by means of these meetings [Donald Munro's], an uncommon awakening took place among the people, which was attended with trembling and distress

of body, and some were even constrained to cry out. These emotions were like summer showers, which move about, when the rain falls on one field without a drop on another. They were here today, and in another place tomorrow.'

The Rev. Donald Ross was now beside himself. He received the support of the local gentry in complaining to the proprietor, Lord MacDonald, asking that such gatherings be suppressed on the grounds that they were an 'infringement of his privileges', as well as 'subversive of all public authority'. It was even suggested that the offenders should be ejected from their holdings. However, this did not occur.

This awakening lasted for some two years. Although it had started in the north of the island it quickly spread to other areas. Wherever Donald went the kind of events detailed above followed. For a time at least three or four were converted at every meeting over which he presided. He seemed to carry the spirit of revival with him. However, Donald's constant watchwords during these days were – *'not by might nor by power but by my Spirit'*.

In relation to the Durinish area of north west Skye during the revival one eye witness records:

'It was often a stirring sight to witness the multitudes assembling during the dark winter evenings – to trace their progress, as they came in all directions across moors and mountains, by the blazing torches which they carried to light their way to the places of meeting.'

Another commented:

'There was here then such power with the word of God as can scarcely be believed by Christians who did not witness it, or feel it experimentally.'

The converts of the revival, as might be expected, were looked upon as 'fanatics' and it is reported, 'No gentleman associated with Donald Munro'.

Once asked by a protagonist, 'Who will be the deepest in Hell?' Donald answered, 'Graceless ministers.' But despite the violent opposition of unbelieving clergy, the people took Donald's side. It is even reported that the people ordered two 'Moderate ministers' from a house in Earlish one evening when it was discovered that their only object in being present was to scoff at the blind evangelist.

One of the consequences of the 1812–14 revivals was an 'abandonment of ordinances, as administered by the paro-chial clergy'. Vast numbers of people were attracted to the revival meetings and 'the churches were in consequence very much forsaken'. Consequently, the clergy hit back by refusing the people 'sealing ordinances'. It subsequently became 'evidence of seriousness not to apply to the clergy – or a mark of carelessness and irreligion when application was made'. It seems a strange comment that in the midst of such a situation 'the good work was not hindered by any division'!

About 1817 the wife of the proprietor of Kilmuir granted permission to some of those converted in the revival to erect a meetinghouse, 'contrary to the general wish of the clergy'. It is also reported:

> 'About 1817 a gentleman who had a small tract of land in the parish of Snizort, divided it in to crofts, or small tenements, which were rented by several serious persons, who were attracted thither from the parish of Kilmuir. They were permitted to build a house for meeting, which will contain about 200 persons.'

Those who met here also reported to 'have other two or three meetings in farm-houses'.

The effect for good on the Island as a result of the revival appears to have been universally acknowledged. Even clergy who opposed the movement were forced to admit that positive results ensued.

At some point prior to 1820 (possibly 1817), Donald had moved into a house provided for him at Snizort. However, this did not dampen his zeal as an evangelist. The people gathered at the recently erected meetinghouse every week and sometimes even daily. The building was reportedly packed on such occasions.

About 1821 another Minister in the Island had a 'new birth experience'. He was the Rev. Roderick MacLeod, son of the parish minister at Snizort. At the time of his conversion Roderick was minister of the mission at Lyndale, part of his father's parish.

It is significant that MacLeod's father did not, as did most of his contemporaries, oppose the revival movement, although many, if not most, did not regard him as being an evangelical.

However, Roderick MacLeod himself now became the butt of much ridicule, particularly in regard to his new friendship with blind Donald Munro whom previously, he himself had so often derided. The men became close friends and it is said that their relationship was as close as father and son. MacLeod's subsequent theology was moulded in this relationship and many nights were spent together discussing spiritual matters. MacLeod's reply to one who mocked his relationship with Donald was, 'I expect to spend eternity in Donald's society.'

In 1823 Roderick MacLeod was appointed to the charge of Bracadale. He remained there for fifteen years and Bracadale, under his ministry, became famous as, 'the birth place of souls'. We will say more about MacLeod in a later chapter.

On one occasion Dr John MacDonald, the 'Apostle of the North' was in Snizort with Rev. Roderick MacLeod. The two men had a debate on a point of Scripture over which they could not agree. 'We shall send for Donald,' suggested MacLeod. Donald duly arrived and told them they were both wrong and gave a different interpretation to which both ministers acquiesced!

The years following the 1812–1814 revivals were, in many ways, years of steady growth and consolidation as far as evangelicalism in Skye was concerned. But, as we shall see in the next chapter, others were also to play a significant role in the religious and social development of the island.

The next major revival in Skye was not to occur until the early 1840s. Sadly Donald Munro would not live to see it for he died in 1830 aged 57. However, his spiritual sons and daughters would be instrumental, not only in that revival, but in revivals throughout the Highlands and Islands and in the New World to which so many Skye men and women were to be dispersed.

Chapter 4

Schools and Schoolmasters

The repression of the Gaelic language by successive British governments did great harm, not only to the culture of the Highlands and Islands but also to the cause of religion and education. The education Act of 1616, ratified in 1631 and 1646, set forth as one of its objects: 'That the Irishe [i.e. Gaelic] language, which is one of the chief and principal causes of the barbarite and incivilite among the inhabitents of the Isles and Heylandis, may be abolished and removit.'

Although the Scottish Parliament passed an Act in 1696 encouraging every parish to establish a school and a suitable schoolhouse for a schoolmaster, progress appears to have been painfully slow.

By 1811 the (SSPCK) had two hundred and ninety schools throughout the Highlands and Islands, teaching almost sixteen thousand pupils. However, it taught only in English.

Some may have had access to education, but the poorer Gaelic-speaking people, who made up the majority of the population, were, for the most part, illiterate. Even if the people could have read in their own tongue, there was little reading material available.

Although Bedel's Irish Bible, in Roman letters, had been printed in 1690 this was only the seventh Gaelic book in print and few could read it. It was not until 1776 that the

SSPCK printed 10,000 copies of the New Testament, which had been translated into Gaelic by James Stewart, the minister at Killin. However, it was not until 1828 that a complete Gaelic Bible went on sale at a price the people could afford.

When The Society for the Support of Gaelic Schools (The Gaelic School Society or GSS) held its first meeting in Edinburgh on January 16th 1811, it was informed that:

'The Highlands and Western Islands of Scotland comprehend not less than one hundred and sixty two parishes. The Islands form thirty-one of these and there are about one hundred and thirty one on the mainland, where the Gaelic language is either preached or generally spoken.'

The same meeting was informed that in the Parish of Kilmuir, Isle of Skye, out of a total population of 3,056, 2,718 were unable to read. From a sample of three Highland and four Island parishes, 19,376 out of a population of 22,501 were incapable of reading either English or Gaelic. This new Society recognised the need to teach the people of the Highlands and Islands in their own tongue and to that end resolved at the same meeting, 'by the erection of circulating schools for the express purpose of instructing them [the people] in the Gaelic language ... to teach the inhabitants to read the Holy Scriptures.'

One of the stipulations of the Society was that 'the teachers to be employed by the Society shall neither be Preachers nor Public Exhorters, stated or occasional, of any denomination whatever'. However, this was a rule that was to be bent, broken and cause great problems from the very outset.

The first meeting of the Society subsequently proposed the formation of five Circulating Schools, one of which was to be in the Isle of Skye.

However, by 1813 the Society would appear to have been operating three circulating schools in Skye. At one of these there were 76 pupils, old and young. One of the scholars was aged 56! Another group of pupils consisted of husband, wife and three children. 'The teacher', reports the Rev. John Shaw on April 13th 1813, 'is employed, almost without intermission, from seven in the morning till ten or eleven at night.'

At Clachan School in the parish of Kilmuir where John Beaton was teacher, there were 160 pupils, 106 of whom had learned to read by April 1813. However, the parish minister Rev. Donald Ross had written to the Society on May 11th 1813 complaining that Beaton had gone beyond his duty and was either 'preaching or exhorting' the people in addition to teaching. Consequently, Beaton, in common with Donald Munro, was suspended by his Society due a complaint made by Ross.

During the summer of 1812 one of the Society secretaries made a tour of the Highlands and Islands. On the afternoon of July 10th he landed at Armadale in South Skye, where he spoke with Lord MacDonald regarding the aims of the Society. MacDonald, 'approved most heartily of the people being taught to read their native language, provided that the teachers kept strictly to the office of teaching'. MacDonald's reference was in regard to the Beaton case and the secretary assured him he would report back to him on the matter.

On his arrival in Kilmuir on July 19th the secretary discussed the issue with Donald Ross the parish minister. Following this interview he was 'fully persuaded that this Schoolmaster had repeatedly broken the resolution' relating to the restriction on a teachers, 'preaching or exhorting', and 'resolved that the previous suspension, by the committee, should not be removed'.

On July 17th the secretary had also visited John Norman MacLeod at Dunvegan Castle with Rev. John Shaw. MacLeod also supported the aims of the Society but, 'considers it of the first importance that the Teachers be confined simply to the teaching of reading'.

The gentry of the day appear to have been afraid of something and it cannot be without significance that 1812 was the year during which the flame of spiritual renewal had been ignited in north Skye under the preaching of Donald Munro and others.

Writing to the Society on April 14th 1818 the Rev. John Nicolson of Minginish, Skye, states:

'The effects of the Gaelic Circulating Schools are now so well known, and universally acknowledged, that it is almost unnecessary to say anything on the subject. In this very district, I can testify, that a wonderful change has been produced on the habits of the people.'

Penning a letter to the same Society during the same year the Rev. John Shaw of Bracadale records:

'I cannot refrain from noticing what a change has taken place in this parish, in respect of education, and especially the reading of the Scriptures, since I came to it six years ago. Then, hardly a Gaelic bible was to be seen, and scarce one that could read them; now they are in every hamlet, and almost in every house, especially in the Districts where the Schools have been taught; a spring has been given to education in general, which takes such effect, that I am persuaded, in not many years it will be a matter of surprise to find young persons who are unable to read.'

Once the people were able to read there was a great demand for Bibles. Everyone, it appears, wanted to have his or her own copy. Malcolm MacLachlan, one of the Society Missionaries in Skye in 1830, writing to the Society states:

'It deserves to be remarked that the full price was offered in many cases, even when bibles were given gratis. A poor decrepit girl, deprived of the use of her feet, who lives on charity, and has no means of subsistence except what she earns by knitting stockings, crawled on all fours with the price in her hand for a bible. Of course the money was returned, but it would have done you good to see her delight when the blessed volume was put in her hand.'

The dangers faced by some of these circulating teachers were obvious. Often they travelled on the open seas going from place to place and there were occasions on which tragedy struck. Writing a letter of gratitude to the Society in 1831 the inhabitants of Castle, Isle of Raasay, on Skye's east coast, related the sad events surrounding the death of their teacher:

'Upon the 16th ult. he and another man, accompanied by his new married wife, left this place by boat to the mainland of Skye, to visit his friends in the Parish of Kilmuir, and on his return on Monday 18th, the boat was lost in the Channel, and he and his wife, and the other man, were all drowned.'

However, the social and religious improvement on the Island as a result of such sacrifice, continued. The inhabitants of Culnacnoc, North Skye, in a letter to the Society during 1834 noted:

'Drunkenness, theft, idleness, and dissolute habits in general have been diminished, or have disappeared, where your schools have been situated, whilst there is reason also to rejoice in many conversions to God through their instrumentality.'

The spiritual impact of the work of the Gaelic School Society was now being felt all over Skye. In 1836 the Rev. John Shaw, Bracadale, noted, 'the very children are known to retire for the purpose of private prayer'. One writer, obviously referring to a visit in Shaw's Parish noted:

> 'One man told me, in an affecting manner, that his son, who is only 9 years of age, would insist on his accompanying him in this exercise; and while the child led the devotions together they addressed that God, who, out of the mouths of babes and sucklings, thus perfects praise.'

John Shaw, writing again to the Society states:

> 'I have reason also to believe, that it [the Society] has in an eminent degree the countenance of the King of Kings. It has had a principal lead, I am convinced, in promoting that sense of Divine things, and that attention to the Divine word and ordinances, which, I am happy to think, is beginning to pervade this part of the Hebrides, more especially those spots where the efforts of the Society have been longest and most powerfully exerted.'

Shaw's observations were perfectly accurate and prophetic. The countenance of the King of kings had indeed been turned upon the Gaelic Schools of Skye. Now, that same King was, as is so often His wont, to choose a humble instrument through whom to channel his blessing. That instrument was to be none other than a poor teacher of the Gaelic School Society.

Chapter 5

The Old Soldier

Norman MacLeod was born at Burnal in Minginish, Isle of Skye, in 1773, joining the Army as a young man. On March 8th 1801 we find him in Egypt having joined the 42nd Highland Regiment under the command of General Abercrombie. So fearless a soldier was he that in action against French forces it is recorded that he sat in the bow of the boat through a hail of bullets from the shore. However on the 21st of the same month he was 'dangerously wounded at the battle of Alexandria in which Abercrombie was mortally wounded'. It is reported that Norman's head was almost cleft in two by the sabre of a dragoon! He bore the scar for the rest of his days. Soon after this event, Norman left the services of the Army and took up residence in Edinburgh where he later married.

Norman MacLeod next comes to our attention, sometime between January 1807 and 1813. Walking in Edinburgh one day the words 'Ceannich Biobull' (Buy a Bible) came to him. He obeyed the prompting and as a consequence became concerned regarding spiritual matters. He subsequently came under the influence of Dr. John Macdonald, the 'Apostle of the North', who was at the time minister of the Gaelic Chapel in Edinburgh. His testimony later in life was, 'It was in

Edinburgh I was struck with the bullet of love.' The 'bullet' referred to may well have been fired by Lachlan MacKenzie of Lochcarron, as it is thought he was the preacher on the day Norman was converted.

It would appear that John MacDonald was also instrumental in Norman's returning to Skye and his appointment as Gaelic Schoolmaster to Kilmuir. Little is known regarding when he moved to Kilmuir, or how long he remained there. However, in May 1839 he was appointed as Gaelic Schoolmaster to the teaching station of the Gaelic School Society, at Unish, Waternish. His salary was £25.00 per annum, and a long thatched house, one half of which was used as a schoolroom and place of worship, while the other was home to Norman and his family.

On his first Sunday in Unish Norman went to hear the local parish minister a Mr Ried. It is said his preaching was 'dry, and had no attraction for the Lord's people'. Norman never attended again. Murdo MacDonald, the Lewis man, who subsequently succeeded Norman at Unish also attended the Parish Church on his arrival. On coming out of church the minister welcomed him and said, 'I hope you will not be like the Gaelic Schoolmaster who was here before you; he attended church the first Sabbath after he came three years ago, but we have not seen him since.' Murdo replied, 'Surely he took a good supply with him.'

On June 15th 1839 Norman MacLeod opened his School to pupils. During April of the following year it was reported, 'a few individuals in the district appeared to have been awakened to soul concern, and towards the end of August this concern had spread throughout the district'. At this time, 'it was a common thing for the people to cry out in the meetings in apparent distress of mind'. However, this 'awakening' was relatively short lived.

Norman, it appears, was not very popular with the Parish Ministers of the area who 'did all in their power to prevent him from holding meetings'. On one occasion Norman was visited by a retinue of ministers who asked him, 'Why do you hold a meeting here on Sabbath?' Norman replied, 'I hold it for the glory of God.' His apt reply terminated any further interrogation. However, a short time later, on the instructions of the local Presbytery, Rev. John Shaw of Bracadale called on Norman with instructions for him to stop holding services on the Sabbath. Norman refused stating, 'I will not stop till I finish the work the Lord has given me to do.' John Shaw reported back to the Presbytery, 'I would not take the world to stop that godly man.' However, he was eventually forbidden to hold any service at the same time as the parish minister.

By 1842 Norman's period of service at Unish was drawing to a close. The apparent lack of visible spiritual fruit caused him considerable distress and he confessed to having felt 'his spirit unusually moved regarding their state'.

On the last day of the School session, Sunday, May 15th 1842, Norman gathered the people together. He, 'experienced much tenderness of feeling towards them, and observed strong indications of the same among them'.

At 2pm that afternoon they met together for worship, during which there were, 'appearances of unrest one individual having cried out during the service'. In the evening another meeting was held and Norman read from Mark Chapter 11 and made some remarks regarding the parable of the barren fig tree. In the light of his imminent departure he challenged his listeners regarding their spiritual condition. The Rev. Roderick MacLeod describes the scenes which followed:

'The most extraordinary emotions appeared among the people; some wept and some cried aloud as if pricked in their hearts, while others fainted and fell down as if struck dead.'

The meeting carried on throughout the night and the people continued to be affected in the same manner. Instead of leaving on the Monday as he had intended, Norman remained for a further sixteen days holding services, 'reading and praying almost continually'. The people attended the services 'with so little intermission day or night, that he could get only about two hours sleep every morning'.

What took place during the following weeks is best described by the Rev. Roderick MacLeod, who was an eye-witness to these events:

'The state of things at Unish, as may be readily conceived, soon began to be noised abroad; and the consequence was that numbers from various parts of the country were attracted to the scene, many of whom became similarly affected with the rest. It was now judged necessary that the people should have regular preaching, and the immediate vicinity of the village of Stein was the place fixed upon for preaching. The minister of a neighbouring parish, who had been applied to [most likely MacLeod himself], accordingly went on the day preceding that appointed, and was not a little surprised, on coming in sight of the place, at seeing a dense body of people sitting down as if hearing the word. He proceeded to the spot, and found a friend of the cause, an elder of the church, addressing the congregation, and on his concluding, he gave a short address himself, and dismissed them with an intimation that there would be a sermon next day. It appeared that a report had gone abroad that that was the day appointed for the preaching. Next day the crowd was much greater, the appearance of the congregation, and the impressions on many most striking. At the conclusion, a sermon was again intimated for that day week; and when that day came the crowd was immense, no fewer than 50 boats being hauled up on the beach that had come from various parts of the coast opposite and around. The impressions on the hearers still deepened; and a sermon was again intimated for the following day.

On that day the wind was high, and it was thought that the boats would not venture out, yet many did come; but such was the difficulty they encountered, that it gave rise to a suggestion for changing the preaching station, which was accordingly done, and a well known spot, called Fairy Bridge, where three roads now met, was pitched upon as the most convenient place for meeting, and continued to be the scene of a weekly preaching to thousands for about two months, when the advance of the harvest season rendered it expedient to discontinue it.

Multitudes from all parts of Skye, excepting the distant parishes of Strath and Sleat, flocked to Fairy Bridge; and as a proof of one design of providence, in permitting such outward manifestations as took place under the word, it is a fact worthy of notice, that some who never went to hear the gospel in their own parish, were induced, by what they heard was going on, to go many miles beyond to hear it there.

Soon after the awakening broke out in Unish, it appeared also in Geary, another Gaelic School station in Waternish, under Mr Murdoch MacDonald, the teacher there, and also at Glendale in the parish of Diurinish, so that from that extreme and intermediate point, where it first commenced, it proceeded to the right and to the left, till now, in a series of regular successive movements, it has traversed the whole extent of the island, from north to south, yea and beyond, even to the islands of Eigg and Rhum, in the parish of Small Isles, the most distant bounds of the Presbytery of Skye.'

In September 1842 Dr John MacDonald, the 'Apostle of
the North', made a preaching tour of North Skye. It was his
opinion that the revival on the Island 'exceeded in intensity
and extent anything of the kind in modern times.'

By 1843 it was judged that the results of the revival were
'real and enduring' and that 'on the most reliable information, that there are few families in the whole Island of Skye,
containing a population of 25,000 souls, where there has not
been one or more individuals seriously impressed'.

In the same year we find Norman MacLeod in North Uist.
In a report to the Gaelic Schools Society in January 1844, the
Rev. Norman MacLeod of Trumisgarry, Noth Uist, wrote:

> 'He [Norman Macleod, Skye] had scarcely set his hand to
> the work when several, especially among the young,
> became sensibly distressed at his meetings under
> conviction of sin, and their lost condition. From this as
> a centre point, the revival has been spreading south and
> north ... Persons of all ages and sexes are affected; but
> the majority are within the period called the prime of
> life. In this parish particularly, numbers of children,
> from eight to fourteen years of age, are impressed; and it
> would be an affecting sight to see their parents, as I have
> more than once seen them, carrying them out of the
> meeting-house, apparently lifeless with exhaustion and
> overpowering feelings. Respecting the bodily emotions
> exhibited by the impressed, I would only observe that
> they are similar to those of such as were visible subjects
> of revival lately in Skye, and in several other parts of
> Scotland, in recent as well as more remote periods. We
> have every reason to hope that many, besides those
> visibly impressed, are partakers of the spiritual benefits
> of his merciful visitation. There is reason to fear, how-
> ever, as has often been the case in times past, that
> numbers of those who now seem promising will fall

away; yet the practical effects of the work are highly gratifying, and unquestionably evidence of its heavenly origin. Gross sins are abandoned – carnal levities are given up. A deep and general interest is felt and shown in what is important and saving in religion.'

During one of Norman's visits to Uist, the parish minister, Finlay MacRae warned his congregation against going to hear him, stating that, 'he was only an old soldier'.

Norman MacLeod appears to have continued as a Gaelic teacher in various parts of the Island. He spent his latter days on a croft in Waternish, near the scene of the earlier awakenings. It is reported that Norman was over six feet in height, straight and handsome to the end of his days. He was also a 'melodious singer' as well as a poet.

On visiting Waternish in 1855, an Inspector of the GSS found the teacher, Norman MacLeod, 'a very old man, confined to bed'. His son was teaching the school.

On the morning of the day on which he died in 1858, he said to his wife, 'Before this day ends I will be with Donald Munro.' A short time later his wife found him on his knees, by the chair. He died praying in his 85th year.

Another of the many teachers who were to make a significant contribution to the spiritual life of Skye and its sister island, Soay, was Donald MacQueen.

Donald was born near Portree in 1785. He was therefore about twenty years of age when the Isle of Skye was visited in 1805 by John Farquharson.

Donald was well educated by the standard of the day – being able to read, write and understand the current literature. He also had the advantage of being sent to school in Inverness to complete his education.

On returning from Inverness Donald became a 'tutor in gentlemen's families'. During this time Donald Munro was active throughout the villages and townships of the area. At what point or in what manner Donald MacQueen and Donald Munro came into contact is not known, but it is recorded that it was under Munro's influence that Donald MacQueen entered in to that vital and personal relationship with Jesus Christ – which was to change his life for ever.

Donald MacQueen eventually married. It is recorded that his wife, 'who was like-minded with himself' had been converted under the preaching of John Farquharson.

It was the Rev. John Shaw, Bracadale, who was responsible about 1815, under the auspices of the SSPCK, for appointing Donald MacQueen as the first English teacher in the island of Soay.

It is said that in his latter days Donald MacQueen would often speak of the 'happy experiences' of former days, telling of some who 'made great progress in the knowledge and experience of divine things; so much so, that they attained in a remarkable degree to the full assurance of faith.'

On one occasion James Ross, the Free Church minister in Bracadale, asked Donald to read an extract from a book written in 1742 on the life of Mrs. Edwards, the wife of the famous Jonathan (President) Edwards, of New England. Quoting Mrs. Edward's testimony he read:

'I sought and obtained the full assurance of faith. I cannot find language to express how certain the everlasting love of God appeared. The everlasting mountains and hills were but shadows to it. My safety and happiness and eternal enjoyment of God's immutable love seemed as durable and unchanging as God himself. Melted and overcome by the sweetness of this assurance I fell into a great flow of tears and could not forbear weeping aloud. The presence of God was so near and so real that I seemed scarcely conscious of anything else. My soul was filled and overwhelmed with light and love and joy in the Holy Ghost, and seemed just ready to go away from the body. This exultation of soul subsided into a heavenly calm and rest of soul in God, which was even sweeter than what preceded it.'

After reading this extract Donald closed the book and remarked in a calm and non-surprised manner that such testimonies had been a 'common experience with some who were turned to the Lord in Skye'.

On the November 13th 1885 Donald rose from his bed and sat in his armchair. With his Bible in his hand, and about to conduct family worship he left the body and passed forever in to the eternal enjoyments and immutable love of God of which he had been reading a short time before.

Chapter 6

Rev. Roderick MacLeod

Of his first three years in the public ministry of the Church of Scotland, Roderick MacLeod records:

> 'I was a entire stranger to the Gospel scheme of salvation; and no wonder, for the staple theology of Skye preaching in those days was nothing better than scraps of Blair's sermons or some other meagre stuff.'

Some time before his conversion MacLeod was, on one occasion, passing a group of men. One of the number said, 'There goes Black Rory.' Donald Munro, who was standing nearby replied, 'Cease your scoffing of that young man; the day will yet come when you will call him white Rory.'

Roderick MacLeod was born in the family home on his father's farm at Glenhaultin, Snizort, Isle of Skye in 1794. His father Malcolm was the Parish Minister.

Young Roderick would have been about ten years of age when John Farquharson visited Skye and would have been in college in Aberdeen when revival first swept the Island between 1812 and 1814.

Roderick was subsequently ordained missionary of Lyndale and Arnisort, which formed part of his father's parish, on April 13th 1819.

The first act he performed after his induction was in 'assisting his fellow co-presbyters to find their beds' – they were so drunk. Two years later an event occurred which was to have a profound effect on the young minister, for, on February 2nd 1821 his mother, to whom he was very attached, died.

Shortly after his mother's death Roderick visited the Rev. John Shaw at his manse in Bracadale. As he perused Shaw's library his eyes fell on a copy of Bellamy's *Christian Religion Delineated*. 'That is the very book I want,' exclaimed MacLeod. It was, at least in part, as a result of reading this book that MacLeod became concerned regarding his true spiritual condition. About the same time he also read Chalmers' book *Lectures on Romans* which appears to have made an impact on him. Many years later he referred to Chalmers as 'his spiritual father in the bonds of the Gospel'. About the same time it is said that MacLeod had also been impressed at a meeting held by Donald Munro. From all the available evidence it would appear that there were a number of factors at work in MacLeod's life leading up to his conversion.

The resultant change in his life and preaching soon became apparent and was quickly to alienate him from his clerical associates. They now regarded him as a religious fanatic. In later life Roderick stated:

> 'I have never heard any section of this world's society speak of evangelical religion, with greater contempt, or bitterness than moderate ministers did, with whom it was my lot to associate at the outset of my life.'

During Roderick MacLeod's time in Lyndale (1819–1823) Donald Munro had settled nearby and, as we have seen previously, he and Roderick became close friends.

During 1823 John Shaw, the minister at Bracadale, died suddenly. Shortly after his death Roderick MacLeod was presented to the Parish and subsequently admitted on September 24th the same year. He was 29 years old, active, strong and eager to work.

MacLeod's preaching, as well as being evangelical, was calculated to condemn the outward show of religion as practised by the majority of the upper classes. He maintained the necessity of genuine devotion, humility and restraint. He also condemned the oppression of the poor at the hands of the rich. Preaching such as this was sure to win him few friends in the classes amongst whom he had moved hitherto. Indeed, some of these were to become his bitter opponents and were to do all in their power to have him ejected from the Church.

At his first communion in Bracadale, MacLeod made it clear that only the true believers, who were living a consistent godly life, were to be allowed to the Lord's Table. Consequently out of a communion roll of 250, fewer than ten partook of the sacraments.

He also refused to christen the children of all but consistent Christians. Consequently, numerous complaints were made to the church authorities and a case eventually brought to the General Assembly in May 1824.

The Skye Presbytery subsequently took steps to depose Roderick MacLeod but the 'Bracadale Case' dragged on and on in the church courts and subsequent General Assemblies until 1839 when he was completely exonerated. The whole matter, it was discovered, had been orchestrated by a small number of the upper classes and the Presbytery of Skye who were, on the whole, in league with them. The poor and oppressed crofters who made up the bulk of the population had no complaint with their minister. MacLeod's church was in fact crowded every Sunday and many came from neighbouring parishes to hear his preaching. Some people, even young mothers with babies and young children, walked up to 20 miles just to be at his services!

Another bone of contention between MacLeod, his fellow clergy and the landed classes, was that he supported and encouraged the men of the Gaelic School Society who breached convention by preaching and holding services for their people. His strong support for this society is evidenced by the number of letters from him quoted in their Annual Reports. During the General Assembly of 1832 both the Presbyteries of Mull and Lewis brought complaints regarding 'the irregular conduct of certain teachers within their bounds, who have been publicly preaching on the Lord's day and at other times'. MacLeod in contrast supported such men and was willing to assist them in any way he could.

During May 1824, the Rev. Dr John MacDonald (the Apostle of the North), who had first been introduced to the Island by John Shaw, was passing through on his way to St. Kilda. On the 2nd May he preached at Bracadale for Roderick who had left for the General Assembly in Edinburgh. MacDonald noted in his journal:

'Found the congregation assembled – an immense crowd! Oh "whence shall we buy bread", I said to myself, "that these may eat." Preached with considerable freedom, and, I trust, with some effect.'

On another occasion MacDonald travelled to Skye in order to assist Roderick at a communion in Bracadale. As was his wont MacDonald expressed his intention of travelling to a remote part of the island in order to preach to the people. Roderick would go with him! On their arrival they found a good gathering waiting eagerly for the preaching of the Word from the great Apostle.

However, there was also an interdict from the local minister prohibiting MacDonald from preaching. Roderick takes up the story as he told it to the General Assembly of the Free Church of Scotland in 1866:

'The question was, what was to be done? After some consideration Mr MacDonald said – "I think we cannot consider, we are forbidden to pray, though we are forbidden to preach". The Assembly, I suppose, has heard of preaching prayers, – and if ever there was an occasion to justify such a system of prayers, I think you would allow that this was a very proper one, (laughter and applause) and so it was, for the venerable father prayed and preached more of the Gospel than they had heard from their own parish minister all their days (applause).'

Who said these men had no sense of humour?

In a tract, written in 1839, telling the story of the earlier revivals on the island there is also an interesting reference to MacLeod's ministry in Bracadale. It states:

'Under Mr MacLeod's ministry the good work was prolonged. And, from time to time, through his instrumentality, "many were added to the church of such as should be saved". A door was kept open for Mr MacDonald of Urquhart, whose apostolic visits continued to be regularly paid, and whose faithful ministrations, during the whole progress of the work had been evidently acknowledged.'

During 1837 the Parish of Snizort became vacant and the people of the area subsequently petitioned the Home Office to have Roderick MacLeod as their minister. After the usual formalities and a bit of string pulling by his friends, Roderick was presented to the congregation on September 8th 1837.

So large were the crowds that flocked to hear MacLeod in his new parish it was necessary to extend the original Church at Kensaleyre, Snizort, which had been built by his father. A new wing was built at the rear of the building in 1839 increasing the capacity of the building from 500 to 750.

As Roderick started out on his work in Snizort, the meetings, which had been initiated by Donald Munro some years before, appear to have been still flourishing a few miles away. Although Donald had died in 1830 it was noted in 1839 that, 'the meetings are still maintained ... and that they prosper, through the blessing of God'. The same report continues, 'Donald Munro has several worthy successors – places of assembly have been erected, and, from time to time, the "Good Shepherd", by means of the services there engaged in, brings home some lost sheep, and feeds those, who are already in the fold'. These meetings were reported to have been held, in the main, through the week. However, in areas where there were no evangelical minister (most of Skye!) 'the Sabbath likewise [was] appropriated'.

About three years after this was written a spiritual earthquake was to rock the island from end to end, beginning, as were have seen earlier, in Unish, Waternish. Roderick MacLeod, as we have also noted previously, threw his weight behind the revival movement and fully supported the men God was using.

When the revival meetings moved from Unish and Stein to Fairy Bridge in 1842, MacLeod was the principal preacher. Crowds of between five and nine thousand made up of men, women and children gathered there week by week for several months. Oral tradition suggests that MacLeod preached from his horse on such occasions, circling the vast crowd as he did so.

An eyewitness at Fairy Bridge records how he saw, 'the young and the old, male and female, pouring forth from all sides of the land, from hills, and valleys, villages, hamlets and the lonely hut. The surrounding waters too were covered with about fifty skiffs, like the multitudes which dotted the sea of Tiberias, in pursuit of the Lord himself when he was manifested in the flesh. Like the goings up of the Jewish tribes to the great feast at Jerusalem, was the going up of these anxious islanders to the Gospel meeting at Fairy Bridge'.

Preaching at Fairy Bridge one Wednesday MacLeod took as his text, *'Behold I stand at the door and knock.'* All were aware of the presence and power of the Holy Spirit. During his discourse he said, 'Oh, it is not my fear that Christ will not accept you, but my fear is that you will not accept Christ.' As he continued the cries of the people at times drowned out his voice and he was eventually forced to stop preaching.

One young lad who attended the meetings at Fairy Bridge was Sandy MacKay from Harlosh, Dunvegan. He was a shy retiring person but one who was to become renowned for his outstanding Christian character. In later life, speaking to a friend of the Fairy Bridge gatherings, he said, 'There is a spot to which I could point' and then stopped suddenly. The friend added, 'Where you were converted?' Then, in what was, and in some quarters still is, regarded as Island Presbyterian humility, he replied, 'I am afraid that that day has not come.' Another friend asked, 'Was that the day you were justified?' He replied, 'That was the day I deceived myself; but if it were deception, it was very sweet.'

One day, many years later, a stranger called on Roderick MacLeod at the Free Church manse in Snizort. As he entered the building his first words were, 'I feel myself honoured in coming under your roof, Sir'. He then related how as a young lad he had been 'awakened' at the meetings at Fairy Bridge. This man, with whom MacLeod was to keep in contact, was Major Neil MacLeod. He was born in Waternish on August 20th 1825, so was about seventeen years of age at the time of the Fairy Bridge meetings.

Neil MacLeod had left the Island when he was eighteen and subsequently joined the Royal Artillery in 1850. He had a distinguished military career in India, China, Crimea and other places. He gave testimony to many miraculous escapes from the hand of the enemy. He also became a member of the first military Bible class ever organised and was marked as a man of outstanding Christian character.

During June 1842 a Superintendent of the Gaelic School Society visited Skye. On Sunday 31st, he walked from Portree to Snizort (Kensaleyre) to hear MacLeod preaching. Afterwards he noted in his diary:

'Heard Mr MacLeod preach. I never saw such a general weeping and crying in any congregation, as I saw and heard there.'

The following year the same Society was able to report:

'With scarcely an exception, the fourteen schools in Skye all shared in the outpouring of the Holy Ghost. We have received the same assurance of the stability and steadfastness of the characters moulded anew to God and holiness, under the late awakening in this extensive island.'

In the same report, speaking of the Society School in Culnacnoc, North Skye, one of the Inspectors noted:

'About 300 adults attended to see and hear the children examined. When addressing them, there were some bathed in tears, rejoicing; others crying out, being distressed in mind, having not as yet attained to that liberty which is in Christ Jesus.'

During 1843 a number of complaints had been made by antagonistic ministers against society teachers as a result of their preaching and consequently, breaching society rules. But, in this respect, the report for 1844 observed:

'In the excitement of religious controversy which has recently swept over our country like a flood, and while as yet we scarcely mark any ebb of the surge, it were vain to imagine that your teachers could remain placid and passive spectators.'

During September 1842 a communion weekend took place at Snizort. Writing of this event to his own society, James MacQueen, the Baptist minister at Broadford, reported that, 'between 12,000 and 15,000 attended and hundreds fell down as if they were dead'. 'This usually commences', continued MacQueen, 'with violent shaking and crying out, with clapping of hands. Those affected were mostly women and children.' MacQueen himself does not appear to have approved of such phenomenon. However, as we shall see later, his attitude was to change slightly when revival visited his own congregation!

Only eternity will reveal the true numbers brought to saving faith during these months, but the effect was to be felt, not only in Skye but also throughout other parts of Scotland, North America and Australia.

The new wine of this Skye-wide awakening was potent. The old wineskins of the Establishment were failing fast and a year after the revival commenced, they burst. The so called disruption of the Church of Scotland in 1843 may, in many places, have had strong social/political aspects but as far as Skye was concerned there can be little doubt that the impetus was the evangelical awakening that had come to a climax the previous year.

During August 1845, a deputation from the newly formed Free Church of Scotland visited Skye. On the 13th the group met up with Roderick MacLeod at the Sligichan Inn where they spent the night. Next day the group travelled to Dunvegan, where Dr MacKellar preached to about 1100 people in the open air. Although not part of the official deputation, the renowned Dr Begg also appears to have been in the company on that occasion. The day was wet but the people listened attentively. Begg watched as the gathering broke up and the people departed by sea and land. Speaking a short time later to MacLeod regarding the conditions in which the people were meeting, Roderick informed him that he had recently addressed a congregation of some 1500 people near Portree. The place where they had gathered was a virtual bog!

The small deputation including Roderick subsequently travelled to Portree where the Free Church Yacht, *The Breadalbane*, was waiting to take them to Inverness for the General Assembly.

The Assembly at Inverness opened on August 21st 1845, and during the proceedings, Dr Candlish, who had just visited Skye stated:

> 'That for the keeping alive of true religion on that destitute island [Skye], not only now, but in former times, we are mainly indebted under God, not to the ordained ministers, but to a class of men, whom some would set aside as unauthorised. Unauthorised they may have been of men, but the Head of the Church has owned and acknowledged, and blessed their labours; and we cannot but bear testimony to the fact, that it is to the services of the catechists, the Gaelic Schoolmasters, and other agents in Skye, that we are, to a large extent, indebted that things are so favourable to the interests of true religion, as countenanced by the Rev. Roderick MacLeod.'

It would have been interesting if Dr Candlish had told us who the 'other agents' were. They may well have been the Baptist missionaries and Baptist Churches of Skye, who were also very active at that time.

Although the people of Snizort were able, at an early stage, to acquire a site for a Church building, the members and adherents faced cruel treatment as a result of their attachment to the Free Church. During 1846 at least 16 families – all belonging to MacLeod's congregation – were ejected from their holdings.

In 1847 a further thirty families in MacLeod's congregation received notices to quit their holdings – all being tenants of Lord MacDonald.

Free Church congregations throughout Skye faced similar persecution. In a letter that appeared in the Free Church Magazine in 1849 it was noted that:

'Lord MacDonald is understood to have threatened 3000 souls with ejection from Skye next season, and it is very probable that other proprietors meditate similar doings.'

Apart from Snizort, most of MacLeod's preaching at this time was in the open air. At Kilmuir he recalled, 'conducting the whole service under very heavy rain, and at Uig, during a sermon, on one occasion, it began to snow – the fall being so heavy, that at the close, he could hardly distinguish the congregation from the ground on which they sat except for their faces'.

After preaching in his own church at Snizort on a Sunday evening, Roderick MacLeod made the seven-mile journey to Portree, where he 'met the people for worship in a thatched house that had been used for a Gaelic School'. This arrangement continued until 1849, when a minister was appointed to Portree Free Church.

Roderick MacLeod was not only interested in the spiritual health of the people but also had a genuine concern for their social welfare. He was also a strong opponent of emigration and took a keen interest in education. Within a few years of the Disruption, the Free Church in Skye had 26 Schools!

A communion, which took place at Snizort in 1863, was typical of such gatherings at the time. Thursday, July 16th was the 'fast day'. Long before the services were due to start the people had assembled for prayer. Thereafter there were services in both Gaelic and English, the whole proceedings lasting some four and a half hours. Friday was 'The Men's Day', and the church at Snizort, which held some 1200, was packed. Roderick presided and subsequently called upon six or eight men to 'speak to the question', these addresses being occasionally intermingled with prayer and praise.

Sunday dawned bright and clear but with a cool breeze – a perfect day to hold the services in the open air. People began to assemble at an early hour, flocking from the hills, moors, and along the roadways till about 3000 were present. The gathering would have been larger but given the time of year many were working away from home.

An eyewitness at Snizort on July 19th 1863 takes up the story:

'Round the spot where the field preaching was held, the fields and roads were lined with horses and ponies, gigs and carts, and vehicles of every description which were used in the neighbouring bay.

The scene presented at the field-preaching was most impressive; one cannot imagine a finer subject for a painter's pencil, or a poet's pen.

The tent, in which the minister stood was pitched at the foot of a sloping hill, gradually rising in an undulating form till it terminated in a heathery knoll. In a smooth sward in front of a tent, the table covered with clean white linen was prepared. The whole face of the little hill was clothed with people, some lying on the grass and on the slopes of the hill, others sitting on pieces of rock, or stools provided for the occasion. Round the outskirts of the crowd lay the little children, and younger portion of the audience who had come to witness the solemn scene. Within this circle lay the older portion of the people, while nearer the tent sat the catechists and the elders.'

Roderick preached to the congregation outdoors in Gaelic while an assisting minister preached in English inside the church building. At the conclusion of the preaching both congregations met outside for the communion proper. Our eyewitness continues just as the congregation from the church arrived:

'Just as they approached, the invitation to come to the first Gaelic communion table was being issued. After a few minutes of profound silence a venerable old man wrapped in a shepherd's plaid came slowly forward and took his seat. Soon after he was followed by others, who advanced to the tables in the same slow and reverential manner, till it was filled with about forty communi-cants. And, when seated, there was no starting about, nor appearance of thoughtlessness, but each head, wrapped in a mantle or plaid, was bent in solemn reverence, as if engaged in heavenly communion with Him whose death they were met to commemorate.'

Further servings took place in both English and Gaelic, the whole service lasting some seven-and-half hours, after which many retired to the church where the elders conducted a prayer meeting for another two hours. Still others withdrew to the surrounding hills for private prayer.

On occasions such as these young boys from Portree, aware that a good number of horses would be left in a glen nearby but out of sight, made their way to Snizort where they spent the day playing on the animals. One of these young lads, later converted under the preaching of the Rev. John MacRae, was Duncan Campbell. It is said that when passing Snizort in later life he bowed his head in remembrance of it.

Another young man converted under MacLeod's preaching at Snizort was John Campbell. John was born in the parish of Snizort in 1824. At the time of his conversion he and five other young men built a hut in the hills where they could spend time in prayer and Bible reading. John left Skye and moved to Glasgow in 1847 where he was marked as a fine Christian and outstanding man of prayer.

In 1867 Roderick MacLeod travelled on a preaching tour to the Island of South Uist in an open boat. During the return journey the boat and the passengers were caught in a storm for a night and a day. The effects of the soaking left Roderick drained and his general health declined fairly rapidly. He died on the March 20th 1868. On the day of his death, his friend MacDougall of Raasay noted in his diary:

> 'I have lost a father and a friend; a wise and faithful counsellor for eighteen years past; I am not likely to meet another on earth.'

Many, there is no doubt, echoed his sentiments and felt the pain and loss of his passing.

Chapter 7

Eye Witnesses

As revival swept through Skye in the aftermath of events at Waternish, there was a great demand for evangelical Presbyterian ministers to preach to the people. Two of the men who responded to the call were mainland ministers, one from Kirkhill near Inverness and the other a Rev. MacDonald, from Urray, on the Black Isle, also near Inverness. What follows is a record of part of a visit as recorded by the Rev. Donald Fraser of Kirkhill:

'In October, 1842, it was reported that there was a great religious movement throughout Skye, and that there was need for more ministers. Accordingly I went to assist, accompanied with Mr MacDonald of Urray. We found the people ready to assemble in eager crowds on weekdays as well as on Sabbaths, whether the weather was wet or dry. One day in Bracadale the Rev Mr Glass [Mr Roderick's successor] and I wrote to a remote mission station an intimation that we were to preach. The day was so very rainy that we looked for a very small audience, but to our surprise we overtook group after group wending their way wet and draggled. We came to a rather broad and flooded stream, and for a little hesitated whether we should attempt to ford it though mounted on our horses. After crossing we waited to see what the pedestrians would do. They ingeniously formed a chain, linking arm in arm, the strongest men at the head of it towards upstream. They then stepped in, the men first, bearing the force of the stream supported by the rest, leaning against them. They thus diverted the force of the current from the women who formed the lower part of the chain. All got through slowly, but safely, and proceeded a mile further to the church, wet and dripping. The little Church was filled, and where there was such eagerness to hear the word of God, it was to be expected it would make some impression.

So it was, for about the middle of the service, all heads were down, silently weeping, and wiping their eyes, but, one hard-featured old man who though he held up his head, had some tears running down his furrowed cheek.'

Referring to another occasion Fraser, continues:

'On the same day [Oct., 1842], we sent intimation that there would be preaching at Sconser. The day turned out wet and there was no place for the people to sit with any degree of comfort, but on the shingle of the seashore, when the tide was out. For a shelter, and pulpit for the ministers, oars were set upon end and a sail thrown over them.

The Rev Mr Macdonald preached with effect to an eager congregation and we then wished to dismiss them, but they would not go away. They would insist on getting another sermon. I then preached: and after a time the tide was gaining upon us, so that those in front of the tent had to retire by degrees to the sides. Still they would not go away, until I intimated to them that I hoped to preach next day in the Parish Church at Broadford, some eight miles off, where they might go and hear more. This intimation spread, and next day many came great distances to hear; but unfortunately the parish minister would not give the use of the Church on that day, but offered to give it the next day, and word to that effect was sent to those assembling. We were much disappointed as well as they. Among them a boatful of people came from Strathaird, who offered to take us to see the stalactite cave there on condition that we would afterwards preach in their mission Church. We gladly agreed, and set off with them. After a time we landed, the female passengers who ran in various directions intimating that there would be a sermon at three o'clock. At that hour the little Church was crowded. After the sermon, we proceeded to the boat to return to the manse by six o'clock, as had been arranged; but the whole congregation followed us and pled so earnestly for another sermon, many weeping as they spoke, that I agreed to remain, and preached, though at the risk of offending the parish minister, and being denied the use of the Church next day, thereby disappointed hundreds.

The Minister was highly displeased, and went from home next morning without seeing me but left the key of the church. The Church is some distance from the manse, and on arriving at it, we learned that a large congregation had assembled on the previous day, when we had gone to Strathaird, and though disappointed of a sermon they returned this day and crowded the large Church. During the sermon it was necessary to stop twice and sing some verse of a psalm to calm their excited feeling, so impressionable were their minds at the time. What an ordinary congregation would hear with composure, affected them, so that many trembled, others wept aloud, and some fainted. It was altogether a striking scene.'

Rev. James MacQueen was minister of the small Baptist Church at Broadford, Isle of Skye, at the time of the revival, which began about the spring of 1842. The following are extracts from reports which he wrote for the Baptist Home Missionary Society for Scotland:

June – 1842
'As a church we live in love; the people turn out well throughout the station, and although we cannot say that much good is doing, we have reason to believe the Lord has not forgotten us ... '

September – 1842
'I suppose you have heard what has occurred at the other end of the Island. They had the sacrament last week, and, I hear, that between 12,000 and 15,000 attended, and that hundreds fell down as if they were dead. This usually commences with violent shaking and crying out, with clapping of hands. Those affected were mostly women and children. We have had two or three instances of it in this station, and it is likely it will go over the whole Island. I think it better to refrain from these men, and let them alone; if it be of man it will come to nought.'

December – 1842
'I never saw the church so lively and zealous as at present. The Lord has enabled me to labour more during the last quarter than I have done any harvest since I came to Skye. The fields were truly white, and no employment hindered the people from attending. I never saw such a general desire to hear in every part of

the station, and, indeed, through the whole Island. Four persons were baptised since I last wrote to you. I cannot visit one half of the places to which I am invited. This awakening commenced in the north of Skye, by means of a Gaelic schoolmaster. It has extended to all the parishes of the Island. Some who are affected prove by their conduct that they have not known the evils of sin, notwithstanding their agitation. There is, however, a wonderful change in the conduct of the people, and much attention is paid to the word of God. Uig has been deprived of an able and faithful minister [Mr A. Ferguson], who left the world in peace and confidence.'

March – 1843

'Ten persons have been baptised and added to us since the beginning of the winter, some are making application, and a saving change appears to have taken place on several in different parts of the station … As to the revival, things are more moderate. The crying and fainting are dying away in most places, but the desire to hear is the same. The revival has extended to the mainland; in some parishes it is at its height, and the people are carried home in carts.'

As indicated in MacQueen's report, in the summer of 1842, Mr Angus Ferguson, the pastor of the Uig Baptist Church, died. His brother Duncan Ferguson, missionary at Ross on the island of Mull, travelled to Uig in Skye at that time. During his stay on the Island it is reported that he witnessed, 'those contortions and screamings which have been so frequent'. One evening while preaching he was, 'obliged to conclude, being unable to hear his own voice'.

It is interesting to note that John Haldane, who had been responsible, some years previously, for sending John Farquharson to Loch Tay and may well have sent him to

Skye, was in 1842 one of the secretaries of the Baptist Home Missionary Society for Scotland. His brother Robert was the other.

The same document clearly shows that the 'fire' was not restricted to Skye. Reports clearly indicate a 'stirring' in other areas of the Highlands and Islands.

For example, John MacIntosh of Lochgilphead reports of December 1842:

> ' ... We baptised six persons in the presence of nearly a thousand spectators ... There is an uncommon movement and an unsatiable desire to hear. Sinners are awakened, or receive peace of mind almost every week; the houses can hardly contain the hearers.'

Similar entries fill the report for this Society in 1843. However, Peter Grant, Baptist minister at Grantown notes: 'It would appear that the Western Isles enjoy more times of refreshing than other places'.

Just who were these Baptist Missionaries and what role, if any, did they play in the refreshing which was sweeping the Isle of Skye in the early 1840s? We will attempt to examine this question in the next chapter.

Chapter 8

Baptist Mission

Perhaps no group has received less attention in recent times in relation to the spiritual history of Skye than the Independent and Baptist missionaries who were evangelising on the Island from the early 1800s. Indeed, there have been Presbyterian historians who have denied any significant Baptist influence on the Island, but this is a gross distortion of the truth.

Although popular history cites John Farquharson as the first itinerant evangelical missionary to preach in Skye, lesser-known documents reveal that he was not the only such evangelist operating in the Island about that time.

Although the itinerant missionary, who was responsible for baptising a number of the members of Donald Munro's prayer meeting at Snizort during 1805 or 1806, has never been positively identified, it is distinctly possible he was Walter Munro who was to become a Baptist pastor at Fortrose and, later, Inverness.

Munro, who became a Baptist about 1808, is known to have visited Skye as early as 1805. Writing in May 1831, after visiting Portree, where he had preached in both Gaelic and English in the Court House, Munro records:

'I then came to Uigg, my old favourite place, which I have visited regularly for the past twenty-six years. Had I it in my power, I should like to visit it yearly, while I am able to preach. I remember it when there were scarcely any who appeared to have proper views of the plan of salvation ... '

Another Perthshire itinerant preacher, Peter Fisher, who became a Baptist in 1808, found about 20 Baptists in Skye when he visited about 1815. When he visited the Island again in 1822, the number had increased to about 50. All of these would, most likely, have been members of Uig Baptist Church.

Following a number of itinerant preachers having maintained the work at Uig, William Fraser, a native of Strathspey, arrived in 1826 to oversee the work there. He was subsequently inducted as pastor of the Uig Baptist church on July 27th 1828.

The church in Uig, as we have seen earlier, dated from about 1808. Four years later a chapel, capable of accommodating 300 people, was built beside the river Connon, where outdoor baptisms were held. Fraser was a vigorous evangelist and during the first year of his ministry in Skye (1826) the membership of the Uig church grew to about sixty, however, as many as three hundred attended his services.

During the summer of 1828 Fraser visited his home in Strathspey after a time of ill health. Speaking of Skye where the people were continuing to turn out well to hear his preaching, and with 'great attention' he writes, 'nothing can be done without grace, for conversion is the work of God. Oh for the outpouring of the Spirit, that the wilderness may blossom as the rose'.

During Fraser's ministry in Uig some undisclosed event occurred which brought disgrace to the church. The BHMSS report for 1830 records:

'Of late many have emigrated to America and some who were distinguished for their apparent devotedness to God, have been excluded for improper conduct ... In consequence of these distressing circumstances the church has suffered much in public estimation.'

Fraser himself appears to have been less troubled by this event than others, noting:

'This is what must be expected while the devil goes about as a roaring lion, seeking whom he may devour; but still the foundation of God standeth sure. We are apt to be cast down when our sanguine expectations are not realized; but let us take courage, assured that, sooner or later, the seed sown shall produce fruit; and although we should not be the reapers, we shall partake of the joy, and, if faithful, shall not loose our reward.'

Little did Fraser realise just how true his words were to prove – as bear fruit the sown seed would surely do.

Fraser himself left Uig the following year, emigrating to Breadalbane, Glengarry Co., Ontario, where he subsequently exercised an extraordinary ministry. Writing in 1878 he was able to record of revival under his ministry in Canada:

'Hundreds were added in Breadalbane – 100 members in 14 months – and strong churches formed and multi-plied, which are today are thriving and growing fast. Suffice it to say that, on the field of missionary labour, there are at present nearly 20 Baptist churches ... '

James Miller – probably a Perthshire man, followed Fraser in Uig. In 1832 Miller reports, 'Our number is now very small: four dear brethren left us a few weeks ago for America, and our number is reduced to nineteen'. Miller only remained two years in Uig, the society reporting in 1834 that as 'little or nothing had been done in Uig (Isle of Skye) for a considerable time – your Committee, after mature deliberation, resolved to remove Mr Miller, and as the neighbourhood of Oban was considered a desirable station, he was placed there'.

In spite of the above comment, and due to, 'the earnest application of a few brethren who reside in that neighbourhood', Angus Ferguson, a native of the Island of Mull, was sent to Uig in 1836. Ferguson was able to report the following year that:

'I am happy to state that I have more hope of this station than ever, and I firmly trust that my coming to Uigg was of the Lord. Our meetinghouse will accommodate more than 300, yet on Sabbath it does not contain the people ... Since the commencement of the year, I have visited Portree occasionally. The people come out in crowds, so that houses are not easily found to accommodate them ... '

Throughout 1838 and 1839 smallpox and fever ravaged the island claiming the lives of many. During March 1838, Ferguson and the Uig church set apart a day, 'For beseeching the Lord to pour out his Spirit upon ourselves and others.' 'We sought the Lord', he writes, ' by prayer and supplication, with fasting. We confessed our sins and backslidings, and pleaded forgiveness through the blood of Jesus'.

Ferguson records how during this time they experienced much of the presence of the Lord, and although aware of their own sin and shortcoming, 'felt the spirit of adoption, and cried, Abba Father.' He later notes:

'There is at present a great revival in Uig; the appearance is more promising than any I have ever yet seen. I saw a revival in Mull and in different other places, but although the appearance in Mull was truly glorious, and proved so, yet it was not so promising as the revival here ... Sabbath last we had three additions of young but married men. After preaching to an audience of about 400, we went to the bank of a small river in the neighbourhood. The congregation stood silent and composed on both sides ... There is a great reformation in this place ... '

During the same year two society missionaries spent four weeks in Skye, preaching fifty-two times and travelling some 400 miles. On arriving at Uig they 'preached upon the side of a hill, the meeting-house being too small'. In the evening they baptised two women in the presence of a congregation of some 500.

In June the following year Ferguson's letters indicate that the blessing was still flowing. He writes:

'Our congregation upon the Lord's day amounts generally to about 400. Our Sabbath School is also doing well. It has already been a means of a great moral change among the young. Many of them carry their bibles to the fields, and commit passages of it to memory ... '

In March 1840, Ferguson, after a period of prolonged illness, while touring the 'eastern part of my station' (the Kilmuir/Staffin area) was still able to report, 'Large houses, containing two or three hundred, were crowded to excess ... '. Yet, he appears not to have considered this as revival, for he writes in December, after a similar mission in the same area, 'our meetings were well attended and apparently deep impressions made ... Although I have had grief and trouble here, yet, I have also comfort and happiness, and although there is no appearance of revival at present, yet we hope for better days ... '.

During the following year emigration again diminished the membership of the Uig church, and the population round about. 'Eight of our members are going to America, and I calculate that about 600 are to emigrate from my station, which will reduce the number of our hearers,' wrote Ferguson in June of that year.

Preaching to the departing emigrants during September, he notes: 'I never witnessed deeper impressions than among the emigrants when we preached on board the ships'. Speaking of the 'Sabbath School' at Uig he comments, ' . . . they are all prepared for the Kingdom of Christ, as a watch would be which had all the wheels but wanted the mainspring. May the Lord send us a day of power.'

The day of power for which Ferguson longed and prayed was just round the corner, but sadly he would only live to see the dawning of it, for, as we noted earlier, he died in 1842 as a result of catching a bad cold while engaged on itinerant work.

Following Ferguson's death the supervision of Uig Baptist church was passed to a local man, Donald Ross, who continued as 'president' of the congregation until the late 1860s. Ross was a faithful servant who saw congregations of up to 200 during the 1850s.

If itinerant evangelists were active in north Skye as early as 1805–1806 it is almost inconceivable that they were not also active in other parts of the island. Such a conclusion is borne out, at least in part, by the fact that in 1825, there was a firm Baptist presence in Strath, south Skye when James MacQueen, arrived in Broadford as missionary for the Society for the Propagation of the Gospel at home.

MacQueen had been a member of Grantown on Spey Baptist Church, and had been trained as a pastor/evangelist by Lachlan MacIntosh in a class sponsored by Robert Haldane.

Some three years after his arrival in Skye the membership

of the Broadford church stood at 27. However, this number did not reflect the crowds who gathered to hear his preaching. In 1829 the BHMSS was able to record of MacQueen:

'On one occasion after preaching in the afternoon, Mr M. intimated a sermon in the evening, at a little distance. So many people followed him, that the house would not contain the congregation; and as the night was calm, he got a candle to enable him to read the passage to which he referred, and preached for two hours in the open air.'

During 1829 two Baptist missionaries, 'Messer's M'Pherson and Tulloch', toured the south Skye area. In one district, 'where there were a number of small houses, all the inhabitants, amounting to 60, assembled in a few minutes'. The following day and in a different location the men found, 'young and old engaged in the fields; but in the course of half an hour, from 50 to 60 assemble in each place'. The BHMSS report records that 'When Mr Tulloch visited this benighted part of the country fourteen years ago (1814) it was difficult to collect a congregation.'

The following year MacQueen himself was able to report, 'More attention is paid to reading the word of God than for a hundred years back, and the parish is pretty well supplied with scriptures'.

In 1833 James MacQueen was transferred by the BHMSS from Broadford to Lochcarron on the west coast mainland. During the same year there he was preaching to congregations of up to 400. All his services had to be held in the open air, as there was no building big enough to accommodate the gatherings. He also started a Sunday school and a class for people wishing to read in Gaelic.

By 1834 congregations at Lochcarron had increased to

between 200–300 on the Lord's Day and 60–200 on week-days. He writes:

> 'They have no house which can contain the congrega-tion, and are often exposed to the inclemency of the weather ... Late last night I came home from Gairloch, where I spent a Lord's Day with the brethren, who are doing well. No time is better for a tour than winter, for the people are all at home, and have little to attend to. But I endured much fatigue in crossing hills, and going through rivers in snow and rain; however the Lord has preserved me ...'

Visiting Skye in 1835 MacQueen records that his meetings were well attended and that, 'there was a great cry for me to remain among them'. In the light of this and the fact that the work in Lochcarron had not been as promising as expected he returned to Broadford in June the following year. The parting was sore, MacQueen noting: 'I never witnessed such lamentation as on the day I left, but they were comforted when I told them I would visit them as often as possible'.

In the summer of 1838 MacQueen was ordained as 'elder' of the church in Broadford by Alexander Grant, Tobermory and Duncan Ferguson, Mull. Both Ferguson and Grant subsequently preached throughout the island. On June 8th MacQueen and Angus Ferguson, Uig met in Portree and subsequently preached together in the Uig area for about a week before crossing to 'MacLeod's Country' where they found many people 'gathering shellfish, being in great want of food'.

One evening during Grant and Duncan Ferguson's visit to Broadford, a woman who was present at family worship, shared with the gathering, 'very feelingly of what God had done for her'. She confessed that while Duncan Ferguson had been speaking of the preciousness of Christ, she was ready to cry out, 'Truly he is precious to me.' However, she restrained herself. After speaking for a time to those gathered she said, 'Seeing Christ is precious to me, what doth hinder me to be baptised?' Grant replied in the words of Acts 8:37, 'If you believe with all your heart, you may.' 'Yes,' she said, 'I believe and am willing to follow the Lord through good and bad report.' She was subsequently baptised.

On another occasion during this visit they found some fishermen mending their nets for the first time in the season. 'We also', said the missionaries, 'are fishers and are going to set our nets.' 'Perhaps you are like Peter', replied the fishermen, 'you would catch men'. 'They left their nets', reported Grant and Ferguson, 'and heard very attentively'.

Towards the end of the year, in common with the Uig church, numbers attending Broadford Baptist Church increased dramatically. So much so that James MacQueen was able to report in December:

> 'As to the attendance through the station, I could not wish it better; there is a desire to hear, almost in every part. For six weeks back, our congregation has increased greatly. On some Sabbaths our meeting-house could not contain above one half of the people, and last Lord's day, not more than one third of the hearers, so that we had to take to the field. The number of hearers was from 400 to 500; and in the evening, even after dark, many were about the door and windows ...'

This was at a time, it should be remembered, prior to the great Skye-wide revival, which commenced some three to four years later. There is therefore overwhelming evidence to support the suggestion that these Baptist churches were the first churches in Skye, since the 1812–1814 revival, to experience a fresh outpouring of the Holy Spirit.

Nor was the blessing restricted to Skye. When MacQueen visited Lochcarron in December 1838 he notes, 'I have been through Lochcarron and Gairloch; where the people attended better than for years past. On the Lord's Day many came from far to hear, and some appeared much impressed ...'. In June the following year he reports of Lochcarron, '600–800 attended on the Lord's Day'.

Writing in September 1841, as revival showers were again refreshing the Island, James MacQueen was ministering in the north of Skye. He notes:

'At Uig we found two vessels going to America. Most of the emigrants were on board, and the whole country in a very unsettled state, in the view of parting with their friends. On the Saturday we arrived, I preached on board one of the vessels. The people heard with great attention. They thanked me, and said that they hoped they should never forget what they had heard. They insisted that brother Ferguson and I should preach on board on Sabbath. I preached on shore in the morning, and in the evening one of us preached on each vessel to a great number of people. On Monday some of them came ashore, and insisted that we should preach to them again. We preached to them five or six times, and had a good opportunity of conversing with the poor people, and we trust our labour was not in vain.'

During the same year, Angus Ferguson, Uig had informed the BHMSS, 'Emigration to Cape-Breton and Prince Edwards Island is upon a very extensive scale this year. Six hundred have already put down their names and many more intend to go.' Among the emigrants in 1841 were eight members from the Broadford Church and eight from the Uig Church.

We noted in an earlier chapter MacQueen's reactions to

the phenomenon, which began to appear as revival swept through the island in 1842. We have also seen something of the benefits that the church in Broadford reaped as a result of this revival.

During February 1843, Alexander Grant, Tobermory, visited Skye. He reports:

'In compliance with a very pressing request from Mr. McQueen to visit Skye, I went in February [1843] by the steamer to Broadford, and remained during two weeks, preaching through the parishes of Strath and Sleat. The weather was very severe, with heavy falls of snow. We preached once every day, and frequently twice. Owing to the poverty of the people and want of accommodation, we had sometimes to travel seven or eight miles over snow-clad hills; and, after preaching, had to return to Broadford without tasting any thing, except cold water. On one occasion we travelled over a high hill covered with deep snow; the day was soft and rainy, and we had often to wade knee-deep through puddles of snow and water. In crossing a river, brother McQueen was almost carried away with the stream. We had several times to cross stormy lochs in small open boats. One cold night we slept in the same barn where brother A. Ferguson caught the cold, which issued in his death; but the Lord was our keeper. The sun did not smite us by day, nor the moon by night, and we were amply rewarded for all our labour, by seeing so many asking the way to Sion, and the people everywhere flocking to hear the word of God, and listening with great attention. We spent two days at a farm where several members of the church reside, and were informed there were there more than twenty promising converts. Four of the number applied for baptism, and gave ample satisfaction; the baptism of the others was delayed. I was highly pleased with the promising appearances last year, but the prospect is now much more encouraging.'

Reporting of his own work in Skye for the period May 1843 – March 1844, MacQueen writes:

June (1843)

'In former years little could be done in spring, but during the last quarter the people turned out at any time. The desire to hear was surprising, and in most places this still continues. Five persons were baptised and added to us since I wrote you last; some are making application, and a number appear to be brought to the knowledge of the truth.'

December (1843)

'The Lord has done much good in this station during the past year, and He continues to give testimony to the word of his grace. The people, especially the young, turn out well. It is very encouraging to see young people paying such attention to the Gospel. Two years ago, hardly any meetings were held through the country, except by our people; now there are a number of weekly meetings for prayer and exhortation in many parts of the station, by people not connected with us, but favourable to us. I have seen the day which I often prayed for, and I trust it is the beginning of greater things.'

March (1844)

'As a church we live in love; since I wrote to you last, six persons have been baptised, and some are making application. The station is truly promising; many appear to know the truth. During the last quarter I have confined my labours to my own station; I could not think of leaving it, seeing the work of the Lord so promising, and the general desire to hear the truth. Last Sabbath being a fine day, I preached in the open field. Nearly a thousand people attended, and in the evening three hundred. After evening service we had a prayer meeting; the house was crowded. Our Sabbath Schools are doing well, and the brethren are very active in promoting the cause of truth. Our dear brother Grant spent fourteen days with us, and we were greatly refreshed by his preaching and conversation.'

Alexander Grant, Tobermory, was back in Skye again during June 1844. On the 14th he visited a sick woman in Broadford and at her request preached in her house. The following Sabbath he, 'met with the church and preached to about 260 attentive hearers, and in the evening to a large audience'. Grant's account continues: 'So eager were some of the Slate people to hear the evening sermon, that they allowed their companions to take away the boats, and walked home round the end of the loch, a distance of ten miles, over very rugged ground.'

During the potato famine of 1846, James McQueen, Broadford, played a major part in alleviating distress in the area. He was greatly respected, not only as a preacher, but also for his genuine love and concern for the people amongst whom he ministered. Writing in March of that year he records, 'I am seldom at home. I have been for some days employed in visiting the sick and dying, and I trust these visits are blessed to many ... '

Reporting on his work in 1847 MacQueen noted, 'I in general travel sixteen to eighteen miles on Sabbath, and preach twice.' But despite his extensive labours the want of success appears to have weighed heavily on him, as did the destitution and hardship of the people. Writing in June 1848 he seems perplexed as to the attitude of the people in relation to their soul welfare: 'It is truly remarkable that in most places where destitution prevails in the Highlands, callousness in regard to religion prevails to a great degree'. The following year he records, 'There has been much sickness, and, from want of proper treatment, many are great sufferers. Many have died. The people have attended well in almost every part of the station; but to witness their poverty and suffering is truly distressing ... '

By 1852 the outlook for the Broadford Church appears to have been grim. 'As a church we live in love and harmony', writes MacQueen, 'but can say nothing in the way of prosperity in getting additions, for every year our number is decreasing by emigration. It appears likely that six or seven of our members will emigrate this season, some to Australia and some to America; so that I am afraid, in a short time there will be few left, – for destitution prevails, and the people must go where they can get food and employment'.

Returning from a visit to Uig during which he had been accompanied by Duncan Ferguson, Mull, he writes: 'The state of the people as to destitution and want is truly lamentable; and the cry for emigration is astonishing. I am truly afraid that there will be many cases of death by starvation, unless God, in mercy, will do some great thing for us'. This bleak outlook was soon to impact severely on his companion for, on returning to Mull, Duncan Ferguson himself became seriously ill, and, a short time later, his wife died in childbirth, leaving him with seven young children. Yet this man was to press on as a faithful servant of Jesus Christ.

On February 8th 1854, MacQueen reported that his youngest child had been seized with smallpox. On the 20th, the Rev. John MacKinnon, Church of Scotland Minister of Strath, in a letter addressed to the Secretary of the BHMSS, informed them that McQueen himself had succumbed:

'It is with feelings of very deep regret that I have to inform you of the death of the Rev. Mr McQueen of smallpox, on Saturday last. It is very much to be regretted, and by none more than by Mrs MacKinnon and myself, as we always had a great regard for him, on account of his sincere piety, amiable disposition, and unobtrusive manners. He has left a widow and eleven children, all young and unprovided for, except two who went to Australia last year. It is my own and Mrs MacKinnon's intention to apply in every quarter where we think something can be done for them.'

The BHMSS report continues:

'Brother Ferguson, from Ross in Mull, had, by appointment, visited Skye during the Winter [February and March], and was there during Mr McQueen's illness, and at the time of his death. And Brother Alexander Grant, on hearing of his death, went from Tobermory to sympathise with the bereaved widow and family of his beloved brother, and the Church in their affliction ... '

Of his visit to Uig during the Winter of 1854, Duncan Ferguson writes:

'During my stay in Uig, which was three weeks, I preached sixteen sermons – the attendance in general very good. About 200 attended the last Sabbath evening I was there. On that day, I baptised one woman, who confessed to have been under conviction upwards of fourteen years, till at last she could no longer resist. Another woman conversed with me on the road, but the night was dark and stormy, and the roads bad, so that little could be said. She had been at the meeting, having come a great distance. She was in an anxious state of mind, and regretted that I was to leave so soon.'

Following a succession of ministries, the Baptist Church in Broadford finally closed its doors for the last time in 1944 while the Uig church, which had not been appointed another full-time minister since the death of Duncan's brother Angus Ferguson in 1842, appears to have dwindled and died out a short time earlier.

Why did a once vibrant missionary church die out? The reasons are many and varied and beyond the scope of this study. However, the main reason was, no doubt, their relatively small numerical base, and, as we have seen, the devastation of the island caused by emigration.

Despite the fact that there is no distinctive Baptist witness on Skye today, there can be no doubt that men such as MacQueen, Fraser, Ferguson, a host of missionaries and the Baptist community in general, played a valuable and significant role in the spiritual growth and well-being of the island, and, as we shall see later, to mission in the New World.

Chapter 9

The Small Isles

Skye's sister islands, the Small Isles (Eigg, Rum, Canna and Muck) also felt the breeze of the Spirit which struck Skye like a hurricane in the early 1840s. Prior to the revival, Rev. John Swanson, an evangelical, had been minister on Eigg for some three years, with little visible result.

The population of Eigg was predominantly Roman Catholic and 'under the control of the priest'. However, there were some 200 nominal Protestants. While Swanson was preaching on Sunday, August 7th 1842 a cry was heard in the congregation. A widow woman 'was impressed' and the whole congregation noticed her.

Donald MacKinnon, the GSS Teacher (a Gaelic School had been established in June 1842) was present on that occasion, and later wrote, 'I may say the awe of God fell upon all'. That same evening during the service three more women 'cried aloud for mercy' and during the services the following Sunday, 'the cries from the meeting house could be distinctly heard at the distance of half a mile'.

On Sunday August 14th, Swanson preached from Acts 17:3: *'Christ must needs have suffered.'* He later recorded:

'The whole congregation was moved, the house was a place of weeping, as if the promise was literally fulfilled,

"They shall look upon me whom they have pierced and mourn". It was an outburst of the whole, so that no mouth was silent, and no eye dry; old and young mourned together, and the blooming and withered cheeks were all wet with tears. The scene was indescribable, and I sat down mayhap to weep too.'

Writing from the Island on November 25th 1842, Donald MacKinnon reports:

'There are now upwards of forty souls under serious concern on this Island alone, and about the same number in the Island of Rum, they are all awake to the means of grace.'

Nor was the spirit of conviction confined to the Protestant population as we also find reports of Catholics 'coming to hear the Gospel'. Generally, however, most of the islands' Roman Catholics viewed the revival as, 'the work of the devil' and the phenomenon surrounding it as 'the braxy' (a disease which affects sheep – resulting in them falling dead). So violent was the opposition of some of the islands' Catholics that they laid rocks on the path to the meeting-house, resulting in some travellers falling and being injured in the darkness.

MacKinnon's report continues:

'At the meeting house there are generally two kinds of weeping, vis, weeping for fear of hell, by those who are under the spirit of bondage; and others weeping for joy, which is more desirable, and which some of them count their life and health ... Generally the meeting house is thronged on the minister's arrival.'

During 1842 a Gaelic School Superintendent visited the

Small Isles. On landing in Eigg he discovered that the minister was on another Island, but that with his approval, MacKinnon was himself holding meetings. The visitor attended and took part, later noting, 'saw a number of people bathed in tears, listening to the word of God'.

The visiting Superintendent was amazed at the spiritual thirst among the people. He records:

> 'I was but a few minutes here talking with those thatch-ing the house, when all the people of the district assembled and filled the house to excess. I had no intention whatever of opening the bible here, but when I saw the poor people coming without any invitation on my part, though it was in a manner transgressing the rules of the Society, I addressed them – saw a number of old and young very much affected, and some crying out.'

During his visit to the School the Superintendent ques-tioned the children regarding their emotions. He asked some of them, 'Why do you weep?', and received the answer from one, 'Because I am without Christ.' 'How do you know that you are without Christ?' he asked. 'The Scripture tells me that I am by nature without God, without Christ ... ' 'For what end did Christ come in to the world?' 'To seek and save sinners', was the reply. 'Do you love Christ?' 'Oh! I am afraid I do not, I wish I could, but alas, I find I cannot ... ' 'Such', he records, 'were some of the answers given by the children who were awakened'. However, the Superintendent found others who 'have a clear view of the plan of salvation, and consequently are rejoicing in the Lord'. 'I had', he says, 'an opportunity of speaking to both old and young, and, to all appearance, some of every description are converted to God.'

The following year the GSS report noted that the revival was continuing in Eigg. Adults from forty to fifty years of age began attending school and those, 'brought to deep anxiety regarding their eternal welfare show in their life and conversation the preciousness and permanence of the impressions which the Holy Spirit had produced in their minds'.

Commenting on events in the Small Isles, Swanson noted in a letter to the Society in 1843:

> 'Considering the elements which the word had to work on here, that when its power was first felt, that there was a good deal of physical excitement, will not surprise you. But this is gradually subsiding, as the judgement is becoming more enlightened ... I have no reason to despair of any awakened soul ... '

At the time of the disruption in 1843 all of the Protestant population of Eigg joined the newly formed Free Church of Scotland, with the exception of three – 'the servant in the Established Church Manse, the ground-officer on the estate, and his father, a pauper'.

The Island belonged to a Professor MacPherson, Aberdeen, who subsequently refused all requests for a site on which to build a new church and manse. Denied accommodation on the Island, Swanson was forced to leave, along with his family. He made his new home at Isle Ornsay, on the Isle of Skye.

Consequently, and in order to continue his ministry, Swanson procured a small vessel, the *Betsy*, which became his floating manse. In the autumn of 1843 when the General Assembly of the Free Church met in Glasgow, it was announced that the minister of Eigg was coming up and bringing his manse with him! The idea was thought of as romantic by some but when a number went on board they found it to be 'a poor vessel of twelve tons burden, some thirty feet in length, by eleven in breadth, utterly unfit to contend with the storms of the Atlantic.'

One man, who, on a number of occasions, sailed on the *Betsy* with Swanson was his lifelong friend, Hugh Miller of Cromarty. At the time Miller wrote for the *The Witness* and has also left graphic descriptions of his experiences in his book *The Cruise of the Betsy*.

Writing in *The Witness* on April 19th 1845, Miller describes a visit to the Free Church congregation in Eigg:

'The building in which the congregation meets is a low dingy cottage of turf and stone ... We found the congregation already gathered, and that the very bad morning had failed to lessen their numbers. There were a few of the male parishioners keeping watch at the door, looking wistfully out through the fog and rain for their minister; and at his approach nearly twenty more came issuing forth from the place, like carder bees from their nest of dried grass and moss, to gather round him and shake him by the hand ... Rarely have I seen human countenances so eloquently vocal with veneration and love ... The rude turf building we found full from end to end, and all asteam with a particularly wet congregation, some of whom, neither very robust nor young, had travelled in the soaking drizzle from the further extremities of the Island. And judging from the serious attention with which they listened to the discourse, they must have deemed it full value for all it cost them. I have never seen a congregation more deeply impressed, or that seemed to follow the preached more intelligently. ... There was little of externals in the place as can well be imagined. An uneven earthen floor – turf walls on every side and a turf roof above; two little windows of four panes apiece, adown which the rain-drops were coursing thick and fast; a pulpit grotesquely rude, that had never employed the bred carpenter; and a few ranges of seats of undressed deal. Such were the materialisms of this lowly church of the people; and yet here, notwithstanding, was the living soul of a Christian community, understandings convinced of the truth of the Gospel, and hearts softened and impressed by its power.'

Chapter 10

The Wild Man of Ferintosh

The emigrant ship had been caught in a severe storm off the coast of Northern Scotland. The passengers, made up mostly of people from the county of Sutherland, escaping the severe poverty and deprivation of their ancestral homelands, were bound for America.

As the ship, beaten by huge waves, was forced towards the rocks of the northern shore, almost all on board were on their knees uttering loud cries for mercy. Sitting quietly among them was one Kildonan man, James MacDonald. A terror-stricken passenger shouted at him, 'You hardened godless man, why don't you pray?' 'I pity those', came the answer, 'who never prayed till to-night.'

The vessel was dashed on the wild lee shore, but miraculously all on board escaped. The Kildonan man never again attempted to leave his homeland.

In 1770 James Macdonald was appointed catechist for Reay in Sutherland and on November 12th 1779, while engaged in his work at the far end of his parish, his second wife gave birth to her second child – a son – at their home. The only other person present at the birth was a 'pious widow, one of their neighbours'. This child was to become the greatest evangelist the Highland and Islands have ever known and was to exercise a profound influence on the people of Skye.

The widow who had been present at MacDonald's birth took a keen interest in him, and, strange as it may appear to our modern way of thinking, after he had been weaned, insisted in taking him to her own house. MacDonald's parents 'gratified her wish, and he remained for five years under her care'.

Every night, before putting the child to bed, this woman knelt beside him and prayed audibly for him. Such was the impression on his young mind that even in his latter years MacDonald could recollect some of her petitions. These petitions were to be answered abundantly.

As a teenager John MacDonald was known as 'the cleverest scholar in the parish' and as a young man, narrowly avoided conscription at the hands of an unscrupulous recruiting sergeant, being saved only by the intervention of a local minister.

MacDonald left home for college in 1797. While there he excelled in his educational attainments, coming within the first three in all his classes. It was during an interval from college that the young student became concerned in a deep way regarding his true spiritual condition. Many believe this came about as a result of his reading the works of Jonathan Edwards, the famous pastor of Northhampton, USA, who was instrumental in the 'Great Awakening' of 1740.

John MacDonald was eventually licensed to preach on July 2nd 1805 by the Presbytery of Caithness and shortly after his ordination embarked on a Ossianic tour throughout the North West Highlands, at the urgent request of Sir John Sinclair. Although this tour was not primarily for the purpose of preaching, MacDonald used the opportunity to preach in each parish he visited. After having preached at one such service in the parish of Glenelg, just off Skye's east coast, the minister said to him, 'That was a very good sermon, I suppose, but it was quite unsuitable here; for you spoke all day to sinners, and I know of only one in all my parish'!

MacDonald was subsequently ordained as missionary minister at Berridale, Caithness, in September 1806 having been married the previous January. His time here was short for by December of the same year he had moved on, and was inducted as minister to the Gaelic Church, Edinburgh, in January 1807. His leaving Berridale was timely, for as he took a last look at the cottage, in which he and his wife had been living, the roof blew off and was 'strewn in fragments on the ground'.

During his residence in Edinburgh MacDonald passed through some form of experience, which his biographer, Rev J. Kennedy, Dingwall, refers to as, 'an important change'. He also refers to this experience as 'a fresh baptism of the Spirit', the results of which were soon 'apparent in his preaching'.

Soon after this 'change' MacDonald preached one Sunday in Tain, Ross-shire. A man who had walked some sixteen miles to hear his own minister, Dr MacIntosh, was less than pleased to find a 'smart looking young man walking', as he thought, 'with too rapid progress, and with too light a step towards the pulpit'. This man's testimony continues:

'I felt at once as if the day was lost. I expected no good and shut up my heart against the youth who came between me and my wonted Sabbath fare. He gave out the psalm. "You can't spoil that at any rate", I said to myself. The prayer began; but I scarcely heard the first part of it. Gradually my attention was attracted, but toward the manse seat I found my eye still wandering. Before the prayer was over I ceased to look away from the pulpit. When the sermon began I forgot all but the doctrine I was hearing. As he warmed up with his subject, the preacher became vehement in his action; every eye was riveted on the speaker; and suppressed sounds testified to the effects his sermon was producing. His second discourse was so awe-inspiring that the audience became powerfully affected. Such was the awful solemnity of the doctrine and the vehemence of the preachers manner, that I expected ere he was done, every heart would be pierced, and the very roof of the church would be rent ... '

Such was the preaching of this young man who would one day earn the title 'the Apostle of the North'.

The year 1813 saw MacDonald once again settled in the Highlands. He was inducted to the Parish of Urquhart, near Inverness, the Highland capital, on September 1st that year. He was 34 yrs of age when he came to Ross-shire and within the first year his wife died. The weekend following her death he was due to take a communion in his own Parish. No doubt his elders expected him to postpone the services but he replied, 'No, let not the death of my wife interfere with commemorating the death of my Saviour.'

In the event, as many as ten thousand people, were at 'The Burn', Ferintosh, to hear him preach on the text, *'I will betrothe thee unto me for ever'*. From the very start of the service there was an unusual stillness in the congregation. The preacher's self-denial and sorrow touched the vast crowd. Few eyes were tearless and as evening wore on the groans and cries in the congregation at times drowned out the voice of the preacher. After asking the question from his text, *'Wilt thou go with this man?'* a number of times, a tall middle-aged woman in the centre of the vast crowd stood up, tossed her arms into the air, and exclaimed in tones heard over the vast audience, 'Theid, Theid, O, Theid' ('Will, I will, O, I will'). The preacher replied, 'God grant thee that grace, and to all present here this day!'

It was from his base in Ross-shire that John MacDonald was to embark on long preaching tours throughout the North and West Highlands. A stranger once asked a member of MacDonald's congregation, 'How is your minister?' 'I have neither heard nor seen him for six weeks', was the reply. His long absences, however, were borne well by the majority of his congregation.

During Autumn 1816 MacDonald was on his way to Caithness when some men asked him to preach in the Parish of Dornoch. However, the Parish minister, Dr Bethune refused to allow it. Unperturbed MacDonald and his congregation set off to Riavag in Spinningdale where the un-forbidden ground of Creich touches the boundary of Dornoch. The preacher stood on Creich soil while the congregation sat within the parish of Dornoch. It is reported that he never preached with greater power and a number were 'brought under serious impressions'.

A few weeks after this incident the minister who had refused him permission to preach in his Parish, died suddenly. MacDonald noted in his diary:

'Some weeks ago he refused me liberty to preach on a week-day in his parish though eagerly requested by his people ... The Lord will have his own in spite of all who oppose Him.'

One young man who was among the vast congregation in Riavag that autumn day was seventeen-year-old Alex Murray of Rogart, Sutherland. As MacDonald preached in the power of the Spirit, Alex was so affected that he had to be carried out of the gathering. From that moment until his death at the age of 75, Alex lived an exemplary life – full of the graces of a true Christian.

During 1817 MacDonald spent most of the year preaching away from his home. Some churches locked their doors against him but a few were won over by his kindness. However, others could not be moved to admit the 'Wild man of Ferintosh'.

The presbyteries of Strathbogie and Aberlour subsequently complained to the General Assembly regarding MacDonald's conduct in 'preaching in other parishes than his own' without express permission. Such conduct was deemed as 'irregular and unconstitutional', however MacDonald himself received no official censure.

Some think that ministers of MacDonald's generation had little or no sense of humour. This was certainly not true in his case. Travelling with a fellow minister one day on a ferry, the men were approached by a drunken man with a dog. Lifting the dog to MacDonald's companion the drunk asked him, 'Will you christen this child?' Horrified the minister ordered the man away. Not to be put off the man then turned to MacDonald and presented the dog to him with the same question. Rising from his seat MacDonald said, 'Do you acknowledge yourself the father of what you now present for baptism?' The crowd on the boat who had been watching the episode broke into jeers and the man skulked back to his seat!

It was the Rev. John Shaw of Bracadale, Skye, who first introduced 'the Apostle of the North' to the island and he thereafter became a regular visitor until the time of his death. Given that Shaw died in January 1823, MacDonald had obviously visited and preached on the island prior to that date.

Details of his preaching tours on Skye are fragmented and difficult to trace as none are mentioned in any detail by his biographer. However, we do know that he spent some days on Skye in 1822, probably between September 1st and 4th, while on his way to the distant island of St. Kilda. It is fairly certain that he spent this time in the company of John Shaw, as Shaw subsequently travelled with him on the next leg of his journey to Harris. Shaw had intended travelling to St. Kilda with MacDonald but prior to the journey from Harris to St. Kilda his 'courage failed him', and he returned to Skye.

Following Shaw's death Rev. Roderick MacLeod became minister of Bracadale and it was primarily through him that MacDonald's relationship with Skye continued.

During May 1824 John MacDonald was again in Skye, passing through, once more, on his way to St. Kilda. As we have noted earlier, on May 2nd he preached in Bracadale for MacLeod, where he 'found the congregation assembled – an immense crowd! . . . ' and 'preached with considerable freedom, and, I trust, with some effect'.

On his return journey from St. Kilda in 1827 Macdonald, on Friday, July 21st, stayed the weekend with Roderick MacLeod at his manse in Bracadale and on the Sunday preached to 'an immense congregation', his text being from 1 Corinthians 4:3–4.

It is worth noting that the scenes of John Farquharson's early ministry in Perthshire proved also to be productive soil under MacDonald's preaching some ten years later.

John MacDonald made a number of visits to the places which had been set on fire under Farquherson's preaching, with similar results. During 1816 he was preaching in Gaelic at the Breadalbane communion weekend to vast congregations. On communion Sunday he preached at Ardeonaig on one of his favourite texts – *'Thy maker is thy husband'* (Isaiah 54:5). It is reported that the preaching was accompanied by an extraordinary outpouring of the Spirit. Some of the people could not contain their feelings and cried out – others were bathed in tears while yet others struggled to contain their emotions. Revisiting the area on Friday, September 11th 1835 he noted in his diary: 'Preached at four o'clock at Ardeonaig, a spot once highly favoured to me by various considerations . . . Ah! Ardeonaig! Would these times returned.' They did and vast congregations and similar results again attended his preaching.

The following September found MacDonald back in Breadalbane, where, on Sunday, 11th he preached to a congregation of some 7000. The vast congregation listened with 'earnestness and solemnity'. Many were in tears for the duration of the meeting. The following day the numbers were slightly less but the effects the same. He continued preaching to similar gatherings throughout the area until Monday, September 19th. These were indeed days of revival power and blessing.

During 1842 John MacDonald was back in Skye where he conducted a preaching tour during September of that year. It was most probably he who conducted the Communion service at Snizort where as we have also noted previously between 12,000 and 15,000 attended, and 'hundreds fell down as if they were dead'.

It was in all probability about this time that MacDonald also preached in the Sleat area of south Skye. On one such occasion the people became so agitated that the parish minister, who was in the audience, rose to his feet and warned MacDonald not to 'set the people mad'. However, the warning was ignored and MacDonald continued preaching to great effect. Such a reaction gives us some hint of the emotion and phenomenon which accompanied MacDonald's preaching.

On another visit, during which he stayed at Kensaleyre, Snizort, with his friend Roderick MacLeod, thousands again came to hear him preach. MacLeod rose to introduce his friend to the vast gathering but was doubtful if they could all hear him. Addressing the gathering he said that although they might not be able to hear him speak, when MacDonald rose, they would all be able to hear him! Subsequently, 'The Doctor rose, and with the one gesticulation of holding in the one hand a pocket Testament that he sometimes struck on the other hand, he was easily heard to the outskirts of the great throng'.

During this visit he also preached on the border of Portree Parish, as the incumbent there would not allow him preach within the bounds of his responsibility. At the edge of the crowd was an old man leaning on his shepherd's staff as he listened to the preacher. MacDonald, speaking of the ground on which the sinner may build his hope of salvation, and the relation in which faith stands to the righteousness of Christ, which is that ground, seeing the old man, shouted,

> 'Look at that old man! On what does he rest his weight? His staff on which he leans rests on solid ground! The staff has its own work to do in holding him up. It is by means of it that he leans his weight on that on which it rests. Without a foundation the staff would have no resting-place, and without the staff, which holds him up as he bends over it, he would fall. So it is by faith that a sinner rests on the righteousness of the Son of God!'

On another occasion MacDonald was returning home to Ferintosh, fresh from scenes of revival in Skye. He sent word ahead that he would preach at Invermoriston and on arrival addressed the people at a sheltered spot in the open air. An eyewitness records of that occasion:

> 'He ... preached with great power, from the words of Paul to the Philippian jailer. The impression of that day was extraordinary. The place was like a battlefield strewn with the dead and dying. Not a few survived to testify that the Lord was of a truth present that day'.

While MacDonald would never have claimed to have the gift of prophecy or what may now be termed 'words of knowledge' there was more than one instance when he revealed a supernatural knowledge of the mind of his listeners. One such occasion was during an open-air communion service at The Burn of Ferintosh. A young man had determined in his mind to stand up at the end of the service and proclaim to all what a great sinner he was. Consequently, when the service was over he rose to speak, but before he could utter a word MacDonald rose to his feet again, and pointing to him said, *'Ghille, tha rud agam ri'radh rint. An rud a cheil Dia na cuir thus' an ceill agus thoir so leat, "Glanaidh fuil Iosa Criosd a Mhic sinn o gach uile pheacadh"'* ('My lad, I have something to say to you. Don't you reveal what God has concealed, and take this with you, "The blood of Jesus Christ, His Son, cleanseth us from all sin"').

What was it like to listen to this prince of preachers? Rev. Allan Sinclair, who was brought up in Glen Urquhart, remembers as a child listening to him preaching in his native glen, during a communion service:

> 'I remember, and ever shall, the thrill of that emotional, powerful voice. I sat in the gallery of the church, in a front seat, while he preached from the words, "We would see Jesus". The thrill of his voice was such that I felt as if raised from my seat by some invisible power, and in danger of falling over the gallery. There was a strange power in the thrill of MacDonald's voice. A minister told us – an aged minister of Christ – that on a certain occasion, while hearing him at Strathpeffer, he never knew the meaning of the passage, "My word is spirit," as he did that day. Such was his emotion, that lest he should disturb the meeting, he rose and retired.'

Another man who heard him preaching as a youth in Perthshire was Duncan Campbell. In old age he recalled of MacDonald:

'It is true that I was young and susceptible, but I think he was, in Gaelic, the most wonderfully eloquent, poetical and mesmeric speaker I ever listened to, and I may add that I heard most of the other Disruption celebrities and afterwards many of England's famous orators, clerical and political ... I do not remember that he ever introduced into his sermons the controversial topics of the day. He spoke more like an inspired evangelist than an ecclesiastical partisan. His presence at a communion always caused a huge multitude from far and near to assemble.'

Whether or not John MacDonald visited the Isle of Skye again after 1842 there is no way of knowing. That he influenced a generation of Skye people for their eternal good is undeniable. He died in his seventieth year in 1849.

Chapter 11

Lewis Mission

A number of the men who caught 'The Flame' in Skye during the early part of the 19th century became instruments of revival in other areas. Nowhere was this to be seen more clearly than in the island that lies to the north of Skye – Lewis and Harris.

The first teacher of the Edinburgh Gaelic School Society School in the Isle of Lewis (1811) was a Skye man – Angus MacLeod. On the first day he had three pupils and on the second twenty. Before long the number had increased to sixty.

Such men, using only the Gaelic Bible as their textbook, began to teach the people, both young and old, to read. Until the arrival of the Gaelic School Societies most Lewis inhabitants were illiterate. In the main town of Stornoway in 1811, out of a population of 2000, 1333 were unable to read.

But the acknowledged 'morning star' of the great revival, which was to spread like a flame throughout Lewis in the late 1820s, was another Skye man – John MacLeod. MacLeod, who was born in Kilmaluag, Parish of Kilmuir, Skye, had himself been converted in the North Skye revival of 1814–1816. MacLeod had started his teaching career with the Gaelic School Society in Waternish, Skye, where 'his labours had been abundantly owned by the Lord'. He came with his family to Galson, on the Isle of Lewis in 1820.

Both John MacLeod and his wife had a deep spiritual concern for the people amongst whom they settled. Consequently, and, once more, in clear breach of the Society's rules, he decided to hold meetings where he could read from the Scriptures and explain them to the people.

As a result he came in to confrontation with the parish minister, the Rev. William MacRae of Barvas. The historian, Norman MacFarlane, records of MacRae, 'His foot for crushing was not a small No. 7, and he put his foot on John MacLeod'. As a result the Gaelic School Society dismissed MacLeod from his post. However, the common people of Galson and Dell reacted differently. They raised enough money themselves to pay his salary and built him a school! As a result 'many were brought to a saving interest in Christ'.

The minister, in retribution, removed 'church privileges' from all John MacLeod supporters! But despite this opposition Barvas became the centre from which revival spread throughout the island. This movement was also accompanied by physical phenomenon and 1822 became known as *'Bliadhna An Fhaomaidh'* – 'The Year of the Swoonings'. At revival meetings those under conviction would cry aloud while others experienced convulsions. Some fell in to trances and other converts while 'in a state of physical prostration', experienced visions from 'the unseen world'. Other strange and inexplicable phenomenon also accompanied this revival.

Opposition was fierce and every device was employed to try and suppress the movement. Neil Murray, the Ness teacher who had also been dismissed from his post and Findlay Munro of Tain, a travelling evangelist who visited Lewis about the same time, were also prominent preacher evangelists during the revival.

In a letter to Mr Adam, the local Factor, on December 23rd 1823, the parish minister William MacRae, accused these men of, 'disseminating wild and unscriptural doctrines'. He continues: 'It is easy to see that no good can arise to society from raving effusions of such ignorant men, who with the consummate effrontery assume the character and office of public instructors and expounders of scripture, and by whom the poor people are but too easily deluded'. He ends his letter by encouraging the Factor to 'take an opportunity of checking this growing evil'.

The parish minister of Uig, Lewis, Rev. Alexander Simpson, was also becoming increasingly alarmed. In a letter written to the same Mr Adam on February 5th 1823, he refers to 'that religious phrensy, which, I am sorry to say, has become prevalent of late, and which, if not checked in time, is likely to be attended with most melancholy consequences'. He goes on to call for action by the authorities and requests the arrest of 'a lad from Carlarnish' (Murdo MacDonald from Callenish, who the people regarded as a prophet) who had 'harangued' the people the previous Sunday following the minister's sermon. He also requested a legal order banning any preaching or explaining of the Scriptures other than by the 'constituted authorities'.

Simpson goes in to graphic detail to enforce his requests. There is little doubt that many today would be equally appalled and alarmed at the scenes he witnessed. On the previous Sunday he describes how he was forced to preach out of doors due to the vast congregation. During the service he records, 'I was shocked to see a young woman from Carlua several times seized with spasms, convulsive fits, and screaming aloud in all the wildness of despair'. The result of these letters and their requests are not known.

Despite this kind of phenomenon, which was by no mean rare, and clerical opposition, the work spread. When, in 1824, the Rev. Alexander MacLeod from Cromarty, an evangelical minister, arrived in Uig, Lewis, John MacLeod was re-instated as Gaelic teacher in that Parish, although it is uncertain whether his appointment was under the auspices of any particular society.

In 1827, three years after having arrived in Uig, Rev. Alexander MacLeod held his first communion service. Due to 'unforeseen' circumstance, while en route to St. Kilda, John MacDonald (the Apostle of the North) arrived on the scene. As MacLeod was ill at the time John MacDonald took the various services.

On Sunday, June 24th 1827, MacDonald preached to a congregation of at least 7000 people. The scene it is said was 'indescribable'. This was the catalyst for a great work of Revival. Many it is recorded 'went to their homes rejoicing because of all the wonders they had seen in their midst'. John MacDonald's simple testimony was, 'The occasion was a season of awakening to some, and of refreshing to others, and to myself.'

In 1828 the Revival movement became more widespread. It appears that physical and other manifestations continued to accompany this movement. One later commentator refers to such phenomenon as 'mass hysteria' – 'a device of the enemy'. However, evangelical opposition to this kind of phenomenon appears to be of a later origin and little condemnation can be found in contemporary records, although some who were not familiar with or had first hand experience of this revival did voice their concerns.

By 1828 one historian records that 'the whole Island seemed to be moved with one great and powerful emotion'. The number attending the communion services in Uig, Lewis, that year was estimated at 9000.

One eyewitness who visited the Uig area remarked, 'at all hours, from eight o'clock at night till one in the morning, he had passed by and overheard persons engaged in prayer'. This revival movement continued for a period of ten years with people converted every week.

The social consequences of a renewed humanity were

enormous and far-reaching. Schools were built and education established. Sobriety, kindness and honesty became the order of the day, as did the liberality of the people. One commentator noted, 'The number of sheep annually lost has wonderfully diminished since the commencement of the revival'! The captain of a ship, which was for a time anchored off Lewis awaiting repairs, noted, 'One hears of religion everywhere, but one sees it here in everything.' He further records that having travelled extensively throughout the island at the time, he had never, outside Stornoway, the island capital, met any intoxication or profanity.

Another Skye man who had a profound influence in Lewis was Braes man Malcolm Nicolson. Although details of his life are scant, it is reported that he 'came under the influence of the truth in a prayer meeting which was conducted by Donald Munro, the blind catechist'.

Nicolson also became a Gaelic teacher in Barvas, but on joining the Free Church at the time of the Disruption in 1843, he was put out of office.

A house was subsequently built for him and as an office bearer in the Free Church at Barvas he continued to 'bear witness as a strong supporter in the cause of Christ'.

The bonds of spiritual fellowship, which were formed between Lewis, Harris and Skye, were strong and abiding. Distance did not pose the same problem then as it so often does now, for it was quite common for the people to walk great distances to share in Christian fellowship, especially at communion seasons.

One Lewis man who often visited Skye was the famed Aonghas nam Beann (Angus of the Hills). Indeed it is said that once Angus had visited Skye he seldom left it.

Angus MacLeod was a simple man who could not even count his fingers, yet he was to become endowed with a deep and profound spirituality. He was a shepherd living in a lonely hut among the hills near Uig, in Lewis.

When the revival came to Uig, Lewis, Angus found himself under deep spiritual concern. He went back to his native hills to spend the days and nights in prayer. Many men in the district did the same. Angus became a channel of the love of Jesus and everyone who met him was aware of it. When engaged in prayer there was little if any hint of the mental defect, which marked him at other times.

On one occasion Angus was attending communion services at Snizort in Skye when the Rev. Roderick MacLeod invited him to the manse. During the meal Roderick said, 'Angus, has not grace greatly honoured you when it brought you to my table?' Angus replied, 'And did not grace greatly honour yourself, minister, when you invited me?'

The Rev. Robert Findlayson, Lochs, Lewis, was interviewing three women on one occasion who were seeking admission to the Lord's Table. One had been converted as a result of hearing Angus in prayer, the second on hearing a neighbour repeating one of Angus's private prayers, and the third under Findlayson's own preaching. 'I see,' said Findlayson, 'that I have only one share in this work.'

It was the testimony of Rev. Murdo MacAskill when speaking of Angus that, 'this poor witless man could claim more spiritual children in the parish of Lochs than all the ministers who had preached there in his generation.' No one who met him was allowed to walk away without an answer to the question, 'Do you love the Lord Jesus Christ?' All who came in to contact with Angus were aware of an indescribable power and influence. He lived under the anointing of the Holy Spirit.

Another son of Lewis who had close bonds with the people of Skye was Murdo Macdonald. He is reputed to have been one of the first of three people to be converted through the instrumentality of the Gaelic School Society in Lewis. Murdo, a weaver from Stornoway, was a deep thinker and could be severe in his criticism. One day, at a prayer meeting in a schoolhouse, Murdo prayed that God would remove by death or in any other way the 'feather-bed shepherds who fed not their flocks' – a bold prayer indeed. When the minister of Uig, Lewis, died that year, and the Stornoway minister drowned the following, MacDonald was accused of killing them!

Murdo MacDonald's last journey was to Skye to visit blind Donald Munro. When they met they enjoyed sweet fellowship together. However, his journey to Skye had taken its toll and Murdo began to realise he may not see his native island again. A few days before he died he was concerned as to the place of his burial. 'You shall rest in my own lair', Donald assured him, 'and we shall rise together.' Murdo died in Donald's arms. Both men are buried in the same grave on St. Columbus Island at Skeabost, on the Isle of Skye.

Chapter 12

The '59 Revival

Writing in 1860, the 'prince of preachers' C.H. Spurgeon noted:

> 'The times of refreshing from the presence of the Lord have at last dawned upon our land. A spirit of prayer is visiting our churches. The first breath of the rushing mighty wind is already discerned, while on rising evangelists the tongues of fire have evidently descended.'

What has been termed 'The Second Evangelical Awakening in Britain' followed hard on the heels of a similar revival in Ireland, which in turn had followed revival in America. The story of Jeremiah Lanphier and the midday prayer meeting, which he initiated in Fulton Street, New York, on September 23rd 1857, stands tall in the history of religious revival. As a result of the movement in America it has been estimated that over one million converts were added to the church. In Ireland, following the revival in 1859 the figure was put at 100,000.

News of these revivals also created a hunger in Scotland, and nowhere was this truer than throughout the Highlands and Islands.

However, some two years before Jeremiah Lanphier had started his New York prayer meeting there were indications in Skye of the coming wind of the Spirit, when, during 1854–1855, a distinct breeze was detected among a number of Gaelic Schools.

During the winter–spring, in Stein, Waternish, under the influence once more of the same Norman MacLeod, who had been instrumental in earlier revivals, 'several cases occurred of persons, who were formerly pupils at this and other Gaelic schools, being secretly and silently brought to serious concern, and to seek the way of salvation'.

The Rev. Roderick Macleod, Snizort, himself gives evidence of the effect of the revival, which followed during 1860–1861. In a letter to the Association for the Religious Improvement of the Remote Highlands and Islands in 1862 he records:

'In briefly adverting to the state of some of your schools which I have visited since your last report, I shall restrict myself entirely to their religious condition.

To begin with Arnisort. You are already aware that a religious movement, such as, happily of late, is not uncommon in many other quarters, has more or less pervaded Skye in the course of this year. That movement assumed a decided form in connexion with my congregation, if not actually in the school, certainly in the school-house of Arnisort. It had been customary for some time to read to the scholars accounts of the Lord's work in other parts, and two weekly meetings were stately kept for that purpose, to which any of the neighbours that chose might come.

At the ordinary prayer-meeting held at night on Feb. 1, an unusual number of people, as if moved by a sudden impulse, attended, by which the teacher, Mr. Fergusson, was taken somewhat aback, and feeling rather at a loss what to say, took James's Anxious Inquirer, read the first part of it, and afterwards the 16th chapter of John.

During the meeting an uncommon solemnity was felt; one young girl broke out in cries for mercy, and two young men could hardly stand at prayer; and thus commenced a movement which for many weeks kept the school-house more like a hospital than anything else, many sleepless nights being passed there, and so many going to and fro that it was a matter of wonder and thankfulness that Mr. and Mrs. Fergusson stood it so well. In school the children were often in deep distress at their Bible lessons and in singing psalms and hymns – the latter kindly furnished by your Association.

You will now wish to know what results are observable from all this. Here I beg to be excused if I hesitate to speak decidedly of conversions. I have seen enough of such things to teach me to wait, as "the husbandman waiteth for the precious fruit of the earth, and hath long patience for it, until he receive the early and latter rain". Yet it is worth while telling that forty-six of the scholars under sixteen years of age have been more or less impressed during that blessed season; many of whom are walking so as to inspire the best hopes regarding them. The Lord bless them, and lead them in safety "through the land of deserts and of pits, of drought and of the shadow of death," to a city of rest!

But why should I trespass further on your patience with details of this delightful work? I might tell you much of the children's love of the Bible, which many of them must now learn to read in Gaelic, because in that language they can best understand it; and of their love of the preaching of the Word, to hear which they gladly go any distance, if not through fire, certainly through water, thinking little of walking in an evening from

Arnisort to Portree, at least twelve miles, and returning the same night, cheering each other as they go with singing some of Zion's songs – an instance of which may interest you.

Our friend Mr. McPhail and I were one evening at a meeting at Portree, and on our return hither, while refreshing ourselves with a cup of tea, our attention was suddenly arrested by the sound of vocal music passing the house. Mr. McPhail started to the window and listened till it died away in the distance. It was the Arnisort party, chiefly scholars, returning from the meeting at Portree, and intensely interesting it certainly was to hear a manly voice giving out the line, and then the whole party bursting into full chorus, loud enough to be heard a mile away; at such an hour of night it was even sublime. This may suffice regarding Arnisort; but as it may meet the eye of some who take pleasure in clothing the naked, I beg to add that many of the children were often in deep distress, because their parents would not allow them to come to church in the rags they usually wore.

Your school at Kilmaluag has been visited with a large measure of awakening power. No fewer than ten girls and six boys, one third of the whole number attending, being seriously impressed, and their conduct hitherto is giving general satisfaction, much to the comfort of your worthy teacher there, notwithstanding the amount of labour to which he has in consequence been subjected.

Of your industrial school at Steinscholl, conducted by Mrs. McDonald, the catechist's wife, I have also a gratifying report to make. The school is attended by twenty-six young women, as interesting a looking batch as I ever saw anywhere. Of that number about one-fourth have been so impressed as to give every hope that the true peace of God is in the hearts of some of them at least.

Hitherto in your reports, so far as I know, you could only indulge in expressions of hope regarding the religious condition of your schools; I beg now to congratulate you, and your worthy coadjutors, on the decided proofs which the last season has furnished of the Divine countenance being vouchsafed to your labours of love.'

In Harris also the Gaelic schools played their part during the revival of 1860–1862. Referring to the school in Marig, the Rev. John MacLeod reports:

'Some of the children were deeply affected, and impressed with a sense of their sins, whilst reading their lessons. Parents who were careless about their souls are now seeking their way to Zion, attending regularly on the means of grace, and thirsting for the water of life.'

Commenting on the Skye revival, the Rev. J.S. MacPhail, Benbecula, writing in the Free Church of Scotland monthly on 2nd October 1899, records:

'It, like the others that preceded it, commenced in the north and gradually extended over the whole Island. All the parishes had a time of blessing, and many were gathered to the Saviour, of whom a goodly number remain to this day as living witnesses for Christ.'

Summing up the general feeling throughout Scotland in 1860, the Moderator of the Free Church of Scotland, addressing the General Assembly for that year stated:

'We, as a church, accept the revival as a great and blessed fact. Numerous and explicit testimonies from ministers and members alike bespeak the gracious influence upon the people.'

Chapter 13

Kilmaluag and Strath
1923–1934

Does God favour a geographical location – a community –
one village over another? Could it be that the people of one
area are more favoured by God than another? Or, might it be
that people in one area are more prepared, more open and
more willing to see God move in their community? Whatever our opinion it appears that some communities, even in
Skye, have been more favoured than others.

We have already noted the blessing which was experienced at the School in Kilmaluag, Skye, between 1860 and
1862 under the auspices of the Association for the Religious
Improvement of the Remote Highlands and Islands.

Some sixty years later Kilmaluag was again to be the
location of a discernible move of the Spirit of God, this time
under the ministry of the then Free Church of Scotland
minister the Rev. Kenneth MacRae.

MacRae had arrived in Skye during the winter of 1918–
1919. In a diary entry early in 1923 he reveals the longing of
his heart, writing, 'Oh Lord quicken me! Baptise me anew
with Thy Spirit. Save me from a formal unspiritual ministry'.

In February 1923 MacRae noted in his diary in relation to a
prayer meeting in Kilmaluag:

'The evening was very wet yet about 110 were present, including a car load from Staffin. I had no sooner begun the service than the atmosphere seemed to soften me, and during the prayer I could not keep the tears from brimming over my eyes and rolling down my cheeks. There was something too in the singing that touched me, a soft, gentle, broken note, as though there were a wistful longing among the people for the coming of Emmanuel to bless us ... Throughout the night ... I was repeatedly upon the border of tears. These young people of Kilmaluag seem to draw out my very heart. Surely the steps of the Lord are sounding among us as he draws near to bless.'

During the month of June that same year he notes:

'In Kilmaluag spoke from John 12:21 on the desire of the seeking soul to see Jesus, and had a sweet night. I think the Lord was with us and I have hopes of lasting work having been done. All seemed to be solemnised and some moved.'

Other entries in his diary from 1923 are in a similar vein to those quoted above. However, during October 1923 an incident occurred which was to cause MacRae great concern. For, while he had a burden for revival, he was terrified of the physical phenomenon, which he was fully aware, might accompany such a move of God.

On the evening of Thursday, October 11th 1923, MacRae held a service in the Digg, Staffin, Schoolhouse. There were about sixty people present among whom were three teenage girls. MacRae preached from Revelation 22:17 and 'was given wonderful liberty, clearness of thought and unction of spirit'. 'The breathless silence of my audience told me', records

MacRae, 'that the truth had completely gained the ascendancy over them. If ever I felt the Spirit I did so then.'

At the close of the service one of the young girls 'fell a-weeping'. A short time later as the people were leaving the building MacRae heard a commotion at the door. On investigation he noted the girl 'standing in the middle of the cloak-room, with eyes fixedly staring upwards and with a most heavenly look upon her face, yet unspeakable wistful'. Another girl stood weeping behind her. MacRae approached the girl and spoke to her but her fixed look did not alter. MacRae continues, 'and then from her lips in the most sad, yearning appealing tones I heard the words, "I want to see my Saviour! Oh Christ, reveal thyself to me!" The people were awed, my heart was touched. I succeeded, however, in getting her calmed and taken round to the teacher's quarters, but she trembled all over and appeared to be so weak that she could scarcely walk'.

That night MacRae could not sleep, fearful of a 'general outburst' of the kind of emotion he had just witnessed. He recorded, 'I dread the effect of unrestrained emotion ... I have longed and prayed for a movement. Now, when it appears to be at hand, I dread it'.

Despite MacRae's concern regarding the emotion of others he himself was not immune from the experience. During time in secret prayer and study during May 1923 he records, 'My cup simply overflowed, and so much did I realise His presence that for very joy I could scarcely contain myself'. During the same month he records of a service in Kilmaluag: 'Felt the divine dews fall upon my soul and my hearers seemed to be impressed ... I expect fruit from last night's meeting.'

At the year's end, while preparing a report for the Free Church, he was able, among other things, to note, 'that the average attendance at the prayer meeting [in Kilmaluag] has risen from 7–9 in 1919 to 45–50 in 1924. Apparently therefore we have had what is undoubtedly a revival of religion without being aware of it, a revival which has been entirely lacking in the excitement usually associated with the idea of revival'.

To what extent the 'lack of excitement' was due to MacRae's suppression of what he considered 'unrestrained emotion' we will never know. How the freedom of the Spirit of God and the spreading of this small flame in north Skye may have been extinguished because of such an attitude will also remain a mystery. What is clear, however, is that in later years MacRae continued to oppose any emotional phenomenon accompanying revival.

Writing while minister of Stornoway Free Church in 1940, at a time when revival was sweeping the Island, MacRae noted in his diary: 'I shall give the "swooners" no latitude.' However, some, if not many, of the 'swooners' were to become valued members of his Church and even MacRae was forced to admit that their spiritual experience was genuine.

But, it was not only north Skye that experienced spiritual refreshing during 1923–1924. The man whose name was later to become synonymous with revival in the Island of Lewis was also working in Skye during the winter of 1924. Shortly before he married and initially resigned from the Faith Mission, Duncan Campbell conducted a mission in the parish of Strath, south Skye, where many felt the same breeze of the Spirit.

The early weeks of the mission showed little promise and for the first fortnight average attendances did not exceed thirteen. While visiting in the neighbourhood one woman even slammed the door in his face, saying, 'Clear out, you servants of the Devil!' However, writing for the mission magazine *Bright Words* in January 1925, Campbell noted characteristically, 'But prayer moves the mighty hand of God ...'

In the face of such opposition Campbell and two converts from an earlier mission set to prayer, the two women even praying through the night on one occasion. Slowly but surely numbers increased until nightly attendances were over sixty. The mission lasted some three months and the Spirit of God touched many lives. Duncan Campbell records a number of 'very interesting cases' the following of which is typical:

'We had a cottage meeting in a little township some distance away. A man came to that little cottage meeting, who had not been to church for nine years, but stayed at home singing songs and playing cards with his daughter. The man came to the meeting and went home deeply convicted of sin. He said to his wife, "I must get right with God. I have wasted years in sin." He went up to his room and threw himself on his knees, and, as he said himself, "I prayed till my mouth was dry." He prayed from about ten o'clock till half-past one. Then he threw himself down and said, "If God was prepared to save me, He would have saved me tonight. If I was numbered among those who are elected to be saved, God would certainly have saved me tonight." So he threw himself down in despair. But just then the Lord Jesus Christ Himself drew near, and that verse flashed home to his heart – "If we confess our sins, He is faithful and just to forgive us our sins and cleanse us from all unrighteousness." He jumped up from the couch and called his wife and daughter. "Come up to my room! God has made me a new man!" They prayed and praised till six o'clock in the morning. His wife told me about this great and glorious experience. She said his prayer was wonderful. Two hours after he got saved, he said, "Lord Jesus, I have seen Thy face. I am satisfied with Thy presence. Should you withdraw that presence from me now, until I die I shall never doubt my salvation."'

As a result of these and subsequent missions the work and ministry of the Faith Mission found a special place in the hearts of the Christian community in south Skye, an attachment which continues even today.

That God blessed the ministry of both Duncan Campbell and Kenneth MacRae in Skye during the mid 1920s is beyond doubt. The story of the subsequent Lewis revival in 1949 is well documented, as is the involvement of Duncan Campbell and the Faith Mission. The irony is that Kenneth MacRae opposed the '49' revival, criticised Campbell and even gave a number of public addresses entitled 'Why the Free Church cannot support the Faith Mission'. Apparently theological prejudice knows no bounds!

Chapter 14

The Scattering

'The awakened of Skye are now the good seed of the deserts of America', stated the Rev. John Bonar of Larbert, while preaching in Glasgow in 1840.

The extent, to which the 'good seed' was to influence the religious, to say nothing of the social and economic life, of Canada.

The years of religious revival on Skye were also, as we have seen, years of emigration fever. 'An emigrant ship would come in to one of the lochs by night,' writes one historian, 'and next morning a whole township would be found tenantless, its inhabitants having embarked to seek their fortunes beyond the sea in lands where they should only again in dreams behold the Hebrides.'

The emotion of these partings can only be imagined. One eyewitness in the parish of Strath, in south Skye, told how he,

'could see a long and motley procession winding along the road that led north from Suisnish. It halted at the point of the road opposite Kilbride. And there the lamentation became loud and long. As I drew near I could see that the minister with his wife and daughters had come out to meet the people and bid them farewell. It was a miscellaneous gathering of at least three genera-tions of crofters. There were old men and women too feeble to walk placed on carts. Everyone was in tears; each wished to clasp the hand (of the minister) that had so often befriended them. When they set forth again a cry of grief went up to heaven, the long plaintive wail like a funeral coronach was resumed, and after the last of the emigrants had disappeared behind, the sound seemed to re-echo through the whole valley of Strath in one prolonged note of desolation. The people were on their way to be shipped to Canada.'

Another eyewitness of similar events in Sutherland describes a scene, which must have been as common in Skye and many other places:

'Men, women and children evidenced signs of grief, the sorrow of the women being very loud and open. As the vessel moved away, the pipes played, "We return no more". An old man, a catechist, accompanied the party on board the vessel, and before returning to shore he poured forth a long and pathetic Gaelic prayer ... Most of the passengers had hardly ever seen the sea before, and the gales terrified them. Suddenly, as if by common consent, they raised a Gaelic psalm tune, which mingled, with wild and plaintive effect, with the roar of the surf and wind.'

Donald Martin of Monkstadt, Skye, watched as a child one day as his uncle, the Rev. Roderick MacLeod, boarded an emigrant ship berthed in Uig Bay, to preach a farewell sermon to the tearful crowd. Donald was deeply saddened as he listened to the wailing of those on board. 'I watched that ship', he later wrote, 'as she sailed away, and ever since and now, I have asked myself, and others, the reason why'.

Another man who preached to the departing emigrants was Alexander MacLeod, a missionary of the Highland

Missionary Society, based in Portree. In his journal covering
July 1833 he records:

> 'On 28th July, I went to the ship Adrian, of London, at
> anchor in Portree Harbour, and having on board a great
> number of emigrants. I was desired by the pilot to
> perform worship, to which I immediately consented;
> and although there was a great noise and bustle among
> them when I went on board, I was both astonished and
> delighted to see them behaving with great circumspec-
> tion and attention during the time of worship, after
> which they showed a great desire that I should give
> them another visit, to which I consented. The next day
> being Sabbath, I thought proper to ask the captain's
> permission for other people to come on board, to attend
> worship, which he granted with the greatest pleasure, so
> that on the Sabbath we were on board the Adrian, when
> the deck was greatly crowded.'

The first wave of emigration to Prince Edward Island was
in 1803 when *The Polly*, *The Dykes* and *The Oughton* disem-
barked some 800 Skye folk at Charlottetown.

> 'In the summer of 1828 two vessels sailed from Loch-
> maddy for Canada, with 600 souls on board, and others
> were preparing to follow. In 1829 vessels left Skye for
> Cape Breton; in 1830 the fever of emigration was raging
> in the county of Sutherland, and vessels departed for
> Canada carrying it is said, over 900 persons.'

During the last week of July 1840 a full rigged ship and a
brig left Loch Snizort for Prince Edward Island. The ship
contained 400 people and the brig 200. The brig crossed in
31 days while the ship, due to poor navigation and losing its
way, took 8 weeks. During the journey 9 passengers died on
board the ship and four or five babies were born.

On August 12th 1840 the *Inverness Courier* reported a vessel called the *Nith* was taking out emigrants from the Western Highlands to Prince Edward Island. At Uig, Skye, 400 passengers went on board, and at Tobermory 150. The vessel proceeded to Staffa and Iona, and was going on to the Isle of Man.

On July 6th 1841 the 1660-ton sailing ship *Washington* with a complement of 850 passengers departed Skye from Uig Bay. The majority of passengers were from Snizort, Kilmuir and the East Side of the island. The crossing was completed in a record 22 days, arriving in Charlottetown, PEI on July 28th. Morning and evening worship was held on the Sabbath Day. It is also recorded 'most families kept family worship regularly each day'. Only two people died on this journey.

On June 26th 1841 the bark *Ocean* left Portree with 450 passengers, the majority of whom were from the Isle of Raasay. The journey to Charlottetown PEI took 36 days. The fare was £3.00 sterling with children under 12 travelling for half price. No deaths are recorded, but two children were born en route.

These journeys were, for the age, relatively normal. However, all were not so fortunate. On other crossings smallpox broke out on board and even after enduring the rigours of such a journey the whole Ship's Company found themselves confined in tents on the shores of their 'New World' until the disease had subsided. Hundreds more never set foot on the soil of this their Promised Land.

Among these emigrants were a 'considerable number who had been, converted under the preaching of such men as Roderick MacLeod [Snizort], Dr MacDonald, Ferintosh and Dr Kennedy of Redcastle'. Indeed, Roderick MacLeod's sister Jessie and her husband Donald Murchison of Bernisdale themselves emigrated to Prince Edward Island about 1838. Roderick MacLeod himself visited the Island and while in one home, to the great amusement of the children, came down for breakfast in his bare feet!

Alexander Munro

Alexander Munro, known as *Alasdair Mor na h'urnuigh* (Big Alexander of the Prayers), was born at Kilmuir, Skye in 1774. He was a cousin of the famed blind Donald Munro. Alexander was the Gaelic Schoolmaster, employed by the Society in Scotland for Propagating Christian Knowledge, at Eynort between 1821–1822 and Ferinilea, Bracadale, from May 1821 to November 1832.

In 1830 SSPCK school inspector John Tawse visited Munro. He noted of the school, 'a black hut, no chimney, no furniture, ill-lighted; constant smoke affected the teacher's eyes. The dwelling house was no better'. Of Alexander himself the inspector reported, 'exemplary character but limited literary attainment; useful religious instructor'.

During 1831 Alexander moved with his family to the island of Lewis, where from 1832 to 1838, he served as the SSPCK teacher at Shawbost. It appears that he was superannuated from the society for a time but in 1842 was again in their employ, this time at Bragar. However, the call of emigration had become irresistible and he left Lewis for Prince Edward Island in 1842. The society gave a year's wages to assist him.

Many years later his daughter Mary, relating her experience as a young girl, stated:

'I recall that everyone was talking American and how prosperous their friends there were. There seemed to be dissatisfaction and unrest. Times were hard and getting harder. Finally, after much anxious thought my father decided to sever the age-long tie that bound us to the Hebrides, like oaks to the very ground. We packed the few indispensable worldly goods and started for Prince Edward Island. We were not long in our new homes before father, ever following the lure of education, helped to organise a school.'

Not only did Alexander Munro become a teacher and leader in his new homeland but also organised a Church and preached in it.

At least two of Alexander's sons (he had ten children), Thomas Boston Munro (aged 23) and John (aged 19) had emigrated two years earlier on the Brig *Ruther*. Both became teachers and preachers in their adopted homeland. Thomas subsequently left Prince Edward Island in 1874 with one Donald MacDonald. These men and their families moved to Schuyler, Kansas, USA, where, it is recorded, 'Among the flood of immigrants then pouring into Nebraska, they played an honourable part, and many Churches and Schools in that state are living monuments to the unselfish labour, timely interest, and zeal of the two well educated Skye men, Donald MacDonald and Thomas Boston Munro, and their respective wives and families'. Thomas Munro's son George subsequently became a Congregational minister in Nebraska, where he died in 1914.

Alexander MacLeod

Another Skyeman who was to exercise a considerable influence in Prince Edward Island was Alexander MacLeod. He had arrived on the island during 1839 and put down his roots in Scotch Settlement. Immediately after his arrival Alexander MacLeod took an active part in organising and conducting religious gatherings in a local schoolhouse and private houses in different areas where his fellow countrymen had settled. In the summer months he often preached in the open air or in a grove of woods.

In the summer of 1840 a further group of seventy families joined the new settlement. Among these newcomers were a number of eminent Christians such as one Murdock MacLeod (Murachadh Beag). Murdock was ranked as the first evangelist in Strathalbyn. Both he and Alexander MacLeod, along with John MacNeil, who had been sent to

Cape Breton in 1830 by the SSPCK, but later moved to Bannockburn PEI, were the main instruments in a revival, which swept through the area shortly thereafter. Scores of people who were to become pillars in the church and community ascribed their first wakening to these lay preachers. Such a revival would have coincided with the revival sweeping through Skye and many other parts of the Highlands and Islands at the same time.

In the summer of 1844 the people of Strathalbyn unanimously agreed to commence the building of a church and when the first communion was celebrated in July 1845, some eighty or a hundred sat down to commemorate their Saviour's dying love. Alexander MacLeod was one of three men who were ordained as elders on this occasion.

Samuel MacLeod

Samuel MacLeod was born in Uig, Skye in 1796. He was a Schoolmaster on the Island before he emigrated to Prince Edward Island on board the *Mary Kennedy* on May 31st 1829 at 23 years of age. His father Norman, his mother Mary, and his brothers, Murdoch, Roderick and John, accompanied Samuel.

Prior to leaving Skye, Samuel MacLeod, and no doubt a number, if not all of his family, had become Baptists. As a result of his attachment to Baptist doctrines and his subsequent baptism by immersion, the School Board summonsed Samuel and required him to resign. He is reputed to have been sitting on his own chair during the interview and at the end said, 'I am more independent than His Majesty, our King. If he is dethroned he must leave his throne behind, but I take mine with me.' As he boarded the *Mary Kennedy* the chair was on his shoulder!

There were at least eighty-four family heads on board the *Mary Kennedy*, most of whom were from Uig in Skye. They arrived on June 1st and settled in an area of the Selkirk

Estate, which was later called Lyndale. They named the District Uigg, after their birthplace.

One historian has recorded of this 1829 group, 'Their heritage of piety persisted undiminished for several genera-tions'. Although the majority were noted as 'rigid Calvinists' a small group of MacDonalds, MacLeods, Gordons, Munros and others, were Baptists. It was to the latter group that Samuel MacLeod belonged. He subsequently became the Pastor of this small congregation.

Samuel MacLeod received no stipend and for many years received no payment whatsoever for his ministerial work. At first both the Sunday and weekly meetings were held in houses or barns and were conducted in Gaelic with Gaelic Psalms being sung. However, about 1852 a small wooden church was built to accommodate the congregation.

Despite the fact that the church was small their influence was profound. In the book *Skye Pioneers and The Island*, written in the late 1920s, it is recorded:

> 'So far reaching was the influence of this small Baptist group in Uigg, that neighbours of other denominations testify that throughout their lives they have held the Baptist Church in especial veneration and reverence owing to the irreproachable lives and blameless char-acter of this small group in Uigg assembled about their kinsmen and beloved Pastor, the Rev Samuel MacLeod.'

Another Baptist minister, Rev. Donald Gordon MacDonald, born in Prince Edward Island in 1843 and later of Vancouver, Canada gave the following testimony regarding Samuel MacLeod and the small Church at Uigg:

> 'To say he was a man of outstanding natural ability is no exaggeration. His learning and wisdom were profound; his character irreproachable; his influence widespread;

his example wholesome and contagious. In all my experience of eighty-six years of life, I look back on the character of Rev Samuel MacLeod as one of the most potent and significant things I have met. In speaking of him less than justice would be done were I to refrain from paying, in my own declining years, a final tribute to the memory of the group – the small Uigg group – of MacLeods, Gordons and MacDonalds, who constitute in themselves perhaps the highest expression of the human family that it has been my privilege to know.'

On one occasion two serious minded boys were discussing the day of Judgement. One said to the other, 'Where would you like to be on the day of Judgement?' 'Inside Samuel MacLeod', was the prompt reply. Samuel died in 1881 aged 85 years.

As we have already seen, this drift from native shores had a negative effect on home churches, especially the Baptist churches of Skye which were numerically weak. Most of the members of the Uig, Skye, Baptist Church emigrated to Nova Scotia and Prince Edward Island.

Angus MacLean
Angus MacLean, was born in 'Duthaich ic Leoid' (MacLeod Country) on the Isle of Skye in 1817. The circumstances of his early life are not known but there is little doubt that he had a godly upbringing. It also appears that as a young man he came under the influence and preaching of both Donald Munro and the Rev. Roderick MacLeod, the minister of Bracadale, the parish in which he was born. Donald it is said was 'well versed' in Christian matters. This, along with his 'natural intelligence made him competent to instruct others and fitted him for a career of usefulness in the church'.

In 1841 aged 24 years Angus, most likely in the company of his parents and other family members, left their native shores along with a group of emigrants. They sailed in July from Loch Uig on *The John Walker*.

As already noted, it was on occasions such as this that the Rev. Roderick MacLeod and others would preach to the passengers of the emigrant ships exhorting them to ' "build an altar to the Lord" on their arrival in Nova Scotia.' Indeed, James MacQueen, the Baptist pastor at Broadford, and Angus Ferguson, the Baptist pastor at Uig, record having preached on board such a ship at this very spot some two months later.

The crossing from Uig, Skye to Sydney Harbour, Cape Breton was completed in 21 days.

Angus settled first at Poullet's Cove, later moving to Aspy Bay, Cape North. He married a Portree girl, Ann MacPherson.

These communities were remote even by immigrant standards, situated as they were on the north tip of Cape Breton. For a considerable time the settlers had no communication with the outside world, their communities being self-sufficient. A trackless wilderness of some 40 miles lay between them and their neighbours to the south.

During the winter of 1870–1871 parts of Cape Breton were swept by spiritual revival. Angus entered heartily in to this movement and his meetings, held at North Shore, St. Ann's, were particularly noteworthy. It is reported that numbers of people were converted under his preaching.

Angus MacLean is remembered pre-eminently as, 'a man of prayer'. The Rev. Malcolm Campbell noted of him, 'The gift of prayer was his in fuller measure than that of any man the writer has ever listened to either in pulpit or pew.'

Another records of him, 'I can see him now with my mind's eye as he prayed at the prayer meeting in the Cape North Church in the summer of 1870–71. Surely no man ever besieged heaven as he did.'

Angus died in 1892 aged 75 years. He is buried at Middle Harbor, Cape Breton.

Murdoch Ross

Another Skye family who were to exercise a considerable influence in Cape Breton and far beyond were the Ross's.

Murdoch Ross and his family emigrated from Kilmuir on the Isle of Skye to Cape Breton about 1828, subsequently making their home in the Margaree Valley. Murdoch, who had espoused Baptist principles before leaving Skye was a founder member of Margaree Baptist Church.

Murdoch's sons, Hugh and Malcolm, caught the missionary heart of their father, both becoming pioneer Baptist evangelists in the region – as did one of their close neighbors also from Kilmuir, Alexander MacDonald. These young men travelled incredible distances of foot preaching the gospel and encouraging believers in remote Cape Breton communities.

There was no greater supporter of the work of the Kingdom and the Baptist cause in Cape Breton than Murdoch Ross. During 1848 as his sons were itinerating throughout the island he, although now 63 years old, was not idle, as is evidenced in a letter from his hand, part of which reads as follows:

'Dear Brethren
I have recently made a visit to the churches on the eastern shores of this Island. I spent a few days with the brethren at Mira, whom I had never before seen in the flesh. I find it is immaterial whether we are Scotch-men or Englishmen, if we are only one in Jesus Christ. National attachments, and other things of like kind fall into the shade if only the union of the spirit exists.'

The Spirit that lived in Murdoch Ross lives on today in many of his descendants. Hugh Morrison, present pastor of Margaree Baptist Church, Cape Breton, is a direct descendant of Murdoch as is Allan Ross who is today a missionary among the native Alutiiq people of Kodiak, Alaska.

Donald MacPherson

Little could Donald MacPherson and his wife Sarah have imagined when they left their Skye croft for Cape Breton in 1829, how one of their descendants would shape the spiritual lives of thousands of people throughout North America and beyond. Both Donald and his son Norman were renowned for their godliness. Norman's son George recalled:

> 'My father was a broad-minded man. He loved Christians of every name and had fellowship with all true believers.'

When his wife expressed the wish to be baptised by immersion and join with the small Baptist church in Margaree, Norman, a Presbyterian, did not object, replying, 'If this is your conviction, go on and do what you believe to be your duty.'

However, it was George who was to have the most profound visible effect on the continent of North America.

An outstanding preacher of his generation, Dr Millard A. Jenkins of Abilene, Texas, was to refer to him as, 'easily one of the greatest preachers and evangelical leaders of his generation'.

George was converted in the autumn of 1879 at the age of 13 in Margaree, Cape Breton, during what was to become known as the 'Foster Revival'. As a young man he left home for the mines of Colorado where, in the face of great personal danger and hardship, he was to exercise an incredible ministry as a lay evangelist.

In 1892, at the age of 26, George MacPherson finally attained his lifelong goal and entered Colgate University, New York State, to study for full-time ministry.

At the close of his academic training in 1895, George became pastor of the Mahopac Falls Baptist Church, New York, and immediately saw revival under his preaching.

During the summer of 1902 the work of a tent mission in New York, the Tent Evangel, came to his attention and George decided to visit the city and attend some of the services. This was to be a decisive turning point in his ministry, for the two weeks he spent assisting the Rev. Hartwell Pratt in that mission on West 56th Street between Broadway and Eighth Avenue confirmed his decision to pursue the work of an evangelist. The tent, which seated about five hundred people, was packed every night – not an evening going past without some confessing faith in Jesus Christ.

George MacPherson subsequently went on to become the director of the Tent Evangel, the forerunner of Gospel Tent style mission, reaching out to a worldwide audience.

Writing in 1925 this son of Skye was able to report:

'During the twenty-two years I have had the privilege and joy of serving as director, there has been no abnormal sensationalism, but preaching of the gospel in a sane and moral fashion. When I state, therefore, that we have gathered during this period two million six hundred and fifty thousand souls to hear the gospel, and that many thousands have made confession of faith, and a large number have gone forth to study for the ministry and for the home and foreign fields, it is only done to give the reader an idea of how richly God has set his approval upon the work of the Old Tent Evangel.'

Truly the 'good seed' of Skye, scattered in the 'deserts of America', had blossomed and spread, bearing much fruit.

Chapter 15

The Classroom of History

'Now these things were our examples ...' (1 Corinthians 10:6 KJV). So stated the Apostle Paul of Israel's history, when writing to the early Church. While the study of history may be of great interest it must never be allowed to become an end in itself so far as the Christian is concerned.

The Bible also encourages us to *'Remember the former things, those of long ago ...'* (Isaiah 46:9). There are lessons to be learned, dangers discovered, trends identified and pitfalls, which, in the future, can be avoided, if we are willing to take note. This must surely be true in relation the history of revival in Skye and elsewhere.

Perhaps one of the first questions to be asked is:

What is revival?

> *'Will you not revive us again,*
> *that your people may rejoice in you?*
> *Show us your unfailing love, O LORD,*
> *and grant us your salvation.'* (Psalm 85:6–7)

The word 'revival' can mean various things to different people. It is also a word that has fallen into disrepute in some quarters of the Christian community in recent days.

Some people use the word to describe any evangelistic meeting – but that is not what the word means in its historic sense.

In attempting to analyze revival, different commentators give their own definitions. Historian Colin Whittaker states:

'By revival we mean these special seasons of divine visitation when God by the Holy Ghost quickens and stirs the slumbering church of God.'

But, perhaps one of the most helpful definitions, is given by the late Edwin J. Orr, the renowned revival historian. Orr states:

'The key factor in revival is the outpouring of the Holy Spirit. The outpouring of the Holy Spirit results in the revival of the church. That is the **work of God** with the **response of believers**. The outpouring of the Holy Spirit also results in the awakening of the people. That is the **work of God** with the **response of the people**. The **revived church** then engages in **evangelising** the **enquirers** and in **teaching** the **disciples**, that is **those** who wish to follow, and by many or by few, in the **reforming of society**.'

Each of these key principles can be seen in all revivals, including those throughout the Highlands and Islands during the period we have examined.

Why revival?

'When I was in distress, I sought the Lord;
at night I stretched out untiring hands
and my soul refused to be comforted.

> *I remembered you, O God, and I groaned;*
>   *I mused, and my spirit grew faint.'*   (Psalm 77:2–3)

Why did revival come to Skye when it did? A number of social historians point to the fragmentation of island culture and the breakdown of the old order, as the catalyst for religious revival. While it is not the purpose of this chapter to carry out an in depth analysis of this issue, there is no doubt that there is a degree of truth in such arguments, although they are far from the whole story. The old order certainly was breaking down, life was uncertain, few knew what tomorrow would hold and hardship was the order of the day. Neither were there social services or healthcare, as we know them today.

Although the psalmist agrees that *'It was good for me to be afflicted so that I might learn your decrees'* (Psalm 119:71), many would also turn and curse God in their distress, if indeed they believed in a God at all. There is little doubt that a people who live in prosperity and self-satisfaction feel less need of God than the community in distress. Yet, history proves that God can break in on our affluence – even today and affect communities as they were affected throughout the Highlands and Islands in the past.

Our examination of this subject has revealed that, apart from cultural and social upheaval, there were men and women prayerfully committed to the spiritual welfare of the Highlands and Islands. Such people had a burning passion for, and a deep personal relationship with, their God. Not only so but they were willing to give of themselves selflessly to spread the gospel and if need be to give up everything for their high calling. Perhaps in this, more than anything else, we see the distinction between them and the church today, where the selfishness we find in society at large has become the norm. Many Christians are no longer willing to 'put themselves out'

for the spiritual benefit of others and the cause of Christ's
Kingdom.

God's men

> *'Brothers, think of what you were when you were called. Not
> many of you were wise by human standards; not many were
> influential; not many were of noble birth. But God chose the
> foolish things of the world to shame the wise; God chose
> the weak things of the world to shame the strong. He
> chose the lowly things of this world and the despised things
> – and the things that are not – to nullify the things that are,
> so that no-one may boast before him.'*

(1 Corinthians 1:26–29)

We live in a day when anyone who is to be considered for
what some term 'full-time Christian ministry', is expected to
be highly educated and trained in matters theological. Yet
most of the men God chose to use in the early days of
awakening in Skye would today be passed without a second
glance. In God's eyes, it would appear that the standards of
the Church in our generation matter little.

John Farquharson – a poor uneducated man whom his
tutors had given up as unteachable and Donald Munro – a
poor blind musician are hardly the people the Church would
appoint today if it were considering a major evangelistic
thrust in to a semi-pagan area. Yet these are exactly the men
chosen by God for such a task. Yes – there were to be others
with greater educational ability but even they, before being
used by God, were to become objects of scorn and derision in
the eyes of their clerical peers.

Is it possible that the Church today, with all of its
emphasis on educational ability, and qualifications, has
missed out on the vital importance of the ministry of the

whole body? Might it be that, in a day of moral and spiritual decline, God is calling us all back to the simplicity of true faith, prayer and devotion as we see these qualities displayed in the lives of the men and women we have examined? Is not a heart on fire for God of more importance than any degree, be it from a university or a theological college? Joseph MacKay, one of 'the men' who hailed from Strathhalladale, Sutherland, wrote:

'In times of the prosperity of the church, the Lord's servants ploughed with four horses – faith, love, discernment, and zeal; but as the church declined, faith became lame, love got sick, discernment lost the sight of an eye, and zeal died, so that many do the work with the two horses of carnal reason and human learning.'

None of this is to say that education and theological training do not have their place in the life of the Church. However, education and theology without the life and graces of the Holy Spirit fall far short of God's discipleship requirements. So often, as R.T. Kendall observes, 'our education, culture and refinement stand in the way of the Spirit having his own way'.

Dangers

'It is for freedom that Christ has set us free. Stand firm, then, and do not let yourselves be burdened again by a yoke of slavery.' (Galatians 5:1)

'For the kingdom of God is not a matter of eating and drinking, but of righteousness, peace and joy in the Holy Spirit.' (Romans 14:17)

The Christian New Testament contains a whole letter, the purpose of which is to refute the claims of the legalist on the life and practice of those who had embarked on the journey of faith.

Just as the Judaisers in Paul's day followed him everywhere seeking, 'to spy on the freedom we have in Christ Jesus' (Galatians 2:4), so also in Skye and throughout the Highlands and Islands, similar men followed in the wake of every spiritual awakening. Indeed some were there at the beginning waiting to place the burdens of 'the Law' on the backs of each new convert and seeking to confine and distort the new freedom that they had found in Christ.

This drawing away was to be found even amongst some of the men who had themselves been the human agents in revival. The results can be seen around us today in many churches that are devoid of the freshness and freedom that the Holy Spirit brings.

The suppression of culture

While there is little doubt that many modern historians have exaggerated the negative influence of evangelicalism on Highland culture, there is also little doubt that music, recreation and the arts were targets of disdain and censure by many. While John MacDonald, 'the Apostle of the North', allowed his father to destroy his bagpipes, there is overwhelming evidence that he never lost his love of music, song and Highland culture. Donald Munro may, as some allege, have burnt his fiddle following his conversion, although there is scant evidence for this, but there is no doubt many evangelicals frowned on any form of entertainment whatsoever.

Speaking of the burning of MacDonald's bagpipes the Rev. Norman MacFarlane notes, 'Music has opened many a shut door, and the bagpipes if consecrated to Christ might have drawn Highland hearts in Aberdeen to the Lord'.

Why, we may ask, were these instruments not 'converted' along with their owners? Was the harp of Israel holier than the fiddle of Skye? Was the trumpet of the temple priest used in the worship of the God of Israel any more acceptable to Jehovah than a Highland accordion used in His praise? Perhaps in the initial enthusiasm of conversion, men like MacDonald and Munro looked upon their instruments as idols and as such put them to the flame. However, it is unlikely that every convert regarded his or her God-given talent or the instrument they played, in such a light.

Sabbatarianism

The great theme of the Pharisee, as in the day of the Nazarene, was Sabbatarianism. It is not without significance that Jesus found Himself in more trouble with the legalists of His day regarding this issue more than any other. Such was also the case in Skye and throughout the Highlands and Islands following seasons of revival. This thorny issue has continued to plague evangelicalism in the Highlands and Islands ever since. 'Many of the evangelical ministers of this period favoured a strict code of Sabbath observance', writes one historian.

Then, as now, many and varied Sabbath restrictions were in force. For instance, you could carry a pitcher of water from the door to the fireplace but not from the well. You could brush your coat if it had specks of dust, but you dare not touch your boot if it had a splash of mud.

One of the 'Men' of Skye renowned as a strict Sabbatarian was Angus Munro, a relative of blind Donald and a man who had been converted under his influence. Donald Munro appears to have been wary of this form of extremism and, fearing for his friend in this regard, said to him on one occasion, 'Angus, they will be singing with thee in glory to whom thou wouldest not speak on the road.'

However, of Donald Ross, one of the 'Men' of Lewis it is recorded:

> 'He was a man of big principles and disliked details of application that ware arbitrary and meaningless. He bravely drew fresh water from the well on the Sabbath, and did other things with no local sanction – but no man was more loyal than he to the law of Christ.'

The mother of one Murdoch Stewart, a Catechist from Back, Isle of Lewis, was described as 'a sweet saint and very sunbeam of brightness'. One of her sayings, remembered many years after her death, was, 'My conscience permits me to do today things I could not do twenty years ago, such as carrying peats for the fire through the outer door on the Sabbath day. I don't know whether this shows that I am less spiritual or more spiritual'. There is little doubt as to what some contemporary clerics would have replied!

No wonder Paul instructed, *'... do not let anyone judge you by what you eat or drink, or with regard to a religious festival, a New Moon celebration or a Sabbath day'* (Colossians 2:16).

Violence

Once corrupted by the legalists, the works of the flesh began to replace life in the Spirit. The extreme result of this becomes clear as we later see converts resorting to violence and even attempted murder in their ecclesiastical battles and disagreements. This was seen particularly at the time of the disruption. In Uig, Lewis, for instance, the new minister of the Church of Scotland was attempting to cross from Callanish to Uig, 'when half way over they found the plug had been taken out of the boat and they narrowly escaped being drowned.'

During 1843 disturbances took place in a number of areas. On September 27th the *Inverness Courier* reports riots in connection with church affairs at Logie and Resolis in Ross-shire. The previous Sunday Dr John MacDonald had to go so far as to threaten to, 'refuse all church privileges to such as take any part in creating a disturbance'.

Legalism v. Grace
Legalism and Grace always strive for mastery in the life of the believer. Little wonder that the Apostle Paul reminds us of the importance of standing firm in the freedom Christ has won for us!

The gifts of the Spirit

'Now to each one the manifestation of the Spirit is given for the common good. To one there is given through the Spirit the message of wisdom, to another the message of knowledge by means of the same Spirit, to another faith by the same Spirit, to another gifts of healing by that one Spirit, to another miraculous powers, to another prophecy, to another distinguishing between spirits, to another speaking in different kinds of tongues, and to still another the interpretation of tongues.' (1 Corinthians 12:7–10)

'Quench not the Spirit. Despise not prophesyings.'
(1 Thessalonians 5:19–20 KJV)

While many in the Highland Church today have great difficulty with some of the gifts of the Spirit spoken of here, most of these gifts were in evidence in the Highlands and Islands during the periods we have been examining.

'To another the message of knowledge by means of the same Spirit . . . to another prophecy . . . '
We have already seen displayed in the lives of Donald Munro,

John Macdonald, and others what today, in Charismatic/
Pentecostal circles, would be termed 'a word of knowledge'
and 'prophecy'. While all would agree that the 'forth telling'
aspect of this gift was and is relevant, many are unsure as to
whether or not the gift for today includes 'foretelling'.

In actual fact the men mentioned above were only a
handful of many Christians who, throughout the history of
the Scottish Church, have possessed the prophetic gift in its
'fore telling' aspect. Men of such standing as George Wishart,
John Knox, John Welsh and Alexander Peden, all made
prophetic statements that were literally and accurately
fulfilled. Each of these was also regarded by their peers as
men who possessed the gift of prophecy.

The history of the Highland Church has been one in
which the gift of prophecy has not, by and large, been
despised. It appears to be only in relatively recent times that
prophecy has been held in contempt and consequently the
Spirit's fire extinguished. This is not universally true, as there
is clear evidence within some Presbyterian circles that the
gift of 'prophecy' or 'words of knowledge' are still practised,
albeit in a private and unofficial manner. Two elderly ladies,
who died recently in the Isle of Lewis, were both renowned
for 'knowing the mind of the Lord'. Not only so but they
were sought out by mature Christians of various denomina-
tions for advice and guidance.

There is abundant evidence to prove that these gifts were
much more widespread in the history of Highland Church
than many would wish us to believe.

But it is, perhaps, in the private and devotional lives of
many of these men and women that we see why they lived
in the realms of revelation. The Rev. James Calder, Croy,
(1712–1775) was one who through his diaries reveals the
secret. He would set time apart to seek the mind of God –
fully expecting an answer. Writing on June 24th 1735,
looking forward to the Lord's Supper and feeling his own

unworthiness, he 'resolved to wait upon God for relief ...
and accordingly set some time apart for meditation and
prayer'. Following his confession, God, was, 'graciously
pleased to encourage and satisfy by **suggesting sweetly
and powerfully** that it was His providence and business to
carry the lambs of His flock ... **I laid hold of this promise** in
the Lord's strength, and then pleaded, and still plead its
gracious accomplishment in His time and way'.

On a similar occasion some months later he describes how
he appropriated such a promise, when tempted to doubt:

> 'Because this word was not attended and borne home on
> my mind with that glowing evidence and warm
> emotion of soul which **usually excludes all doubting
> concerning the certainty of the accomplishment of
> the promise, and its coming really from the Spirit of
> God**; because of the want of this, I questioned whether
> it might not be barely from my natural power of
> memory and reflection, or suggested by the enemy,
> and that therefore I had no right to this promise. I was
> resolved of this scruple by considering that faith's
> embracement of the promise, and dependence on God's
> faithfulness for the accomplishment thereof, gives a
> title to the promise.'

Thus Calder, resting in the promises of God revealed to his
own soul, moved forward to revival in his own ministry.

While some may have dreams and others visions it was
through 'impression' that Calder, in common with many
believers, walked in the revelation of God.

'To another speaking in different kinds of tongues ... '

Lachlan MacKenzie, Lochcarron, it is reported, was once
approached by a Skye woman who asserted that she enjoyed
the Pentecostal gift of tongues. MacKenzie is said to have

challenged her to speak in Greek or Hebrew! She declined. However, the same gift was in evidence in Prince Edward Island, Canada, at the time of revival and the language used was indeed believed to have been Hebrew!

While there is much misunderstanding, and no doubt, much abuse surrounding this – the least of the gifts – there can be no doubt that when used by the genuine recipients of it, for the glory of God and the good of the church, it has a valid place and function.

Attitudes to phenomena

As we have seen repeatedly, emotion – even extreme emotion – attended most of the revivals we have examined. Rather than trying to subdue emotion – as more than one contemporary advised – the Apostle of the North, Dr John MacDonald, seems to have encouraged it. At best we can say he did nothing to discourage it. Rev. Roderick MacLeod likewise did nothing to subdue the emotions of the people when the Spirit was at work. Such was the alarm of James MacQueen, the Baptist minister in Broadford, when he heard of the scenes in Snizort, that he determined to have nothing to do with the men involved! Were similar phenomena to accompany preaching today the cry of 'emotionalism' would be heard – not only in every newspaper in the land – but also from many evangelical pulpits. More recent commentators who look for days of revival with little emotion or phenomena have precious few examples to turn to.

It is interesting to note that it was Skye man Ewen Lamont who made one of the greatest defences of the kind of phenomena that accompanied revivals in Prince Edward Island during the same period we have examining. In a book on the life of an island minister, he wrote a chapter of 36 pages defending phenomena, including involuntary motions, dancing, and spiritual ecstasy. He seeks to prove from the Bible and Church history that such phenomena were not abnormal, as critics alleged, but to be expected when the Spirit of God was moving among His people and in the wider community.

If this is true, what are the consequences for a church walking in the power of the same Holy Spirit today?

While Jonathan Edwards cautioned restraint, his advice by no means seeks to scorch the work of the Spirit in this regard. He writes:

> 'It would be very unreasonable, and prejudicial to the interest of religion, to frown upon all these extra-ordinary external effects and manifestations of great religious affections. A measure of them is natural, necessary, and beautiful ... Yet I think they greatly err who suppose that these things should be wholly un-limited, and that all should be encouraged in going to the utmost length that they feel inclined to ... There ought to be a general restraint ... '

Perhaps the words John Wesley once prayed are also worth repeating:

> 'Lord send us revival without the wildfire, but if it cannot come without wildfire, then let the wildfire come too, but by all means, send us revival!'

The greatest of these is love

Many outside the Church look back at the preachers and evangelists of past generations and accuse them of being solely 'hell fire and damnation preachers'. However, a closer look at the record reveals such caricatures to have little basis in fact. While they did not flinch from preaching on the reality of hell and its terror, many of the most prominent preacher/evangelists majored on the love of Christ. There is little doubt that this was due, in no small measure, to their personal experience of this love.

The Apostle of the North, the Rev. John MacDonald, and others, as we have seen, appear to have preached on the love and suffering of Christ more than any other subject. So much was this true of the Rev. James Calder, Ferintosh, who was the son of the Rev. Charles Calder mentioned earlier, that he was known as *'Piobaire na aon phuirt'* ('The piper of one tune'). It is said of this man that he was, 'possessed of ... warm affections, humility, and uncommon modesty, and was one of the most lovable of men'. Yet, there were some who despised his emphasis on the love of Christ and the term used to describe him was spoken in mocking tones. As we have noted earlier, his successor in Ferintosh, the Rev. John MacDonald, was to reap an abundant harvest, much of the seed having been sown during Calder's ministry.

Another friend of John MacDonald who drank deep at the wells of divine love, and saw revival in his parish during 1840, was the Rev. Dr Charles Calder Macintosh, of Tain. Macintosh had, in earlier life, spent time in Skye (circa 1828–1830) where he had been impressed by the attentiveness of the congregations he visited as well as their warmth, freshness and the simplicity of faith exhibited by the young converts.

Macintosh was described by a close friend as, 'the most faultless, humble, loving, and holy man I ever met'. In a sermon preached on the mercy of God, Macintosh concludes, 'I would rather make use of the love of Jesus ... to move, to awaken, to melt, and to draw you. This is the loving Saviour who now invites you – He who wept over His enemies and His murderers. Think what a heaven it must be to be with Him! Think what a hell, were there nothing else in hell, to be separated from Him for ever'.

At a communion in Nigg, Ross-shire a short time before his death, such was the sense of heaven and the grace of God among the congregation, that for many years it was remembered as, *'bord na trocair'* ('the table of mercy').

One man who was converted under his preaching records:

> 'I felt the constraining power of the love of Christ, and was enabled to appropriate Him on the authority of God, in the free offer of the Gospel.'

Macintosh however preached the 'whole counsel' of God, but, when preaching on the reality of an eternity without Christ, 'his fine eye was often filled with tears'.

The Rev. William MacKenzie, who became the minister of Tongue, Sutherland, in 1769 and remained there for sixty-five years, was another Highland cleric who witnessed spiritual revival in his parish. Such was his burden for the spiritual welfare of his people that after four years of apparent fruitless labour, while preaching one morning he, 'burst in to tears and sat down in the pulpit, and for the next five minutes wept and sobbed, his feelings too strong for utterance'. When he at last rose again to preach there was a fresh power apparent and from that day forward, 'there was a fresh outpouring of the Spirit of God'.

For the next several years he never preached on the Lord's Day but, 'as many as six to eight came to him under conviction of sin "asking the way to Jesus"'. One man who knew him intimately asked what were the truths in his preaching which, 'seemed to have been specially blessed for producing this awakening?' 'He told me', writes his friend, 'that the truth which seemed above all others to impress and awaken his people was the dying love of Christ.'

Restoration?

Most of the men and women we have been examining would be appalled if they were to return to the Highland Church today; appalled at the sorry state and depths to which she has sunk; appalled that the gifts and revelation they experienced have, by and large, been relegated to the past and are now opposed by many who claim to honour their memory. They were under no illusion that what they experienced was not biblical. They simply believed the Bible. They believed that the experiences of the New Testament believer and the same revelation given to the saints through-out the Scriptures was also available to them. Was their God not the same God who walked with Enoch of the Old Covenant and Paul in the New? Why should they settle for anything less than God's best?

Appalled they might be – but surprised? Perhaps not! For it was also revealed to many of these believers that the pattern and power of the New Testament Christianity, which they experienced, would not continue. They foresaw decline and grieved over the fact that the vital and experimental Chris-tianity of the Highlands and Islands would soon slip in to a religious formalism – having a name but lacking the power. Revelation would become a bad word and any discussion of dreams, visions or supernatural spiritual experiences would be frowned upon as mere superstition. Men and women would no longer live in the realms of the supernatural and as a result would be devoid of the power and graces of the Holy Spirit.

Consequently for those of us born in the Highlands after the 1940s any memory of a past Highland Christianity, vibrant and moving in the power and revelation of the Holy Spirit, was almost non-existent. For the most part the dead formalism which had gripped the Highland Church since the beginning of the twentieth century was accepted as the norm and nothing to compare it with was known. This is the way it's always been, or so we thought!

Indeed there is clear evidence that some religious historians deliberately hid or deleted references to phenomena or supernatural experience that were contrary to their notions of 'normal' Christianity. Thus a generation was raised in ignorance of their true spiritual heritage. However, these things were not entirely unexpected by previous generations.

An early Highland minister, the Rev. Thomas Ross of Kincardine (1614–1697), who preached in Morayshire and later lived and was imprisoned for his faith in Tain, Ross-shire, stated shortly before he died:

> 'There are very evil days coming that none is like to bide out, save those that have real grace. But I will go off with the faith of it, that Christ shall have a glorious day in Scotland yet.'

The much-revered Dr John Kennedy of Dingwall, also foresaw days of decline; indeed he partly lived through them. In one remarkable sermon on Isaiah 26:20, he predicted the decline of evangelical preaching in the land. The Lord, he remarked, would remove his loving witnesses, and few would arise to fill their place. False but popular teaching would displace the Gospel of free grace, and a generation without spiritual discernment would drink the poison like a blind man would drink unwholesome water out of an unclean vessel. A spirit of worldliness would overcome the people, and the means of grace would be largely forsaken. God's Spirit would be grieved and therefore denied. In such a day the Lord's people would be few and hidden.

Another godly man who lived through more recent years of decline in the Highland Church was the Rev. Murdoch

Campbell of Ness, Isle of Lewis. Preaching in a 'remote congregation' sometime during the early 1950s he records:

> 'My mind was so grieved over the sad state of the Cause of Christ that on the following night I paced the floor of my bedroom in deep concern. Before dawn, however, the Lord composed my spirit in the words of the dying King: "Although mine house be not so with God, yet hath He made with me an everlasting covenant ordered in all things and sure; for this is all my salvation, and all my desire, although He maketh it not to grow" (2 Samuel 23:5).'

Thereafter, the following words were impressed upon Campbell:

> *'Fear not, O land, be glad and rejoice; for the LORD will do great things.'*   (Joel 2:21)

Has the 'sad state of the Cause of Christ' improved in the Highlands and Islands since Murdoch Campbell wrote these words? Few think they have – indeed many, if not most, would agree that the decline has advanced in many parts to a state verging on apostasy.

But the prophetic statements we have quoted hold out a message of hope!

> 'Christ shall have a glorious day in Scotland yet . . . '

> *'Fear not, O land, be glad and rejoice; for the LORD will do great things.'*

At the time of writing these days still appear to refer to the future. Yet, hidden from the natural eye God is at work – breaking down, exposing, but at the same time building up – looking expectantly for the men, women and children who will rise from the ashes of the once glorious Church of the Highlands and Islands with one desire – to be channels, once again, of His Glory to Scotland.

This book is an abridgement of a much larger work by the author. The original manuscript contains the full text of all chapters, additional chapters, source references and photographs.

While the full manuscript is not available in book form a professionally produced multi media CD containing all of the above can be purchased by contacting the author at:

'Shennachie'
Kensaleyre
Isle of Skye
Scotland
IV51 9XF

Tel: +44 (0)1470 532485
Email: Steve@Skye2000.freeserve.co.uk

Alternatively visit the Skye Revivals web site on:

skyerevival.org.uk